NORTHWEST HOMEGROWN COOKBOOK SERIES

Crab

CYNTHIA NIMS

WestWinds Press®

I dedicate this book, and this series, to the memory of my parents,

Bill Nims and Marian Nims. They blessed me with countless gifts, which include

a love of the Northwest, a taste for great food, a passion for finding joy in life,

and a profound sense of what it means to call a place home.

Text © 2002 by Cynthia Nims

Illustrations © 2002 by Don Barnett

Published by WestWinds Press®

An imprint of Graphic Arts Center Publishing Company

P.O. Box 10306, Portland, Oregon 97296-0306

503/226-2402; www.gacpc.com

Library of Congress Cataloging-in-Publication Data

Nims, Cynthia C.

  Crab / by Cynthia Nims.

    p. cm. — (Northwest homegrown cookbook series)

Includes index.

  ISBN 1-55868-601-0 (softbound : alk. paper)

1. Cookery (Crabs) 2. Crabs. I. Title. II. Series.

  TX754.C83 N56 2002

  641.6'95—dc21   2002003174

President: Charles M. Hopkins

Associate Publisher: Douglas A. Pfeiffer

Editorial Staff: Timothy W. Frew, Ellen Harkins Wheat, Tricia Brown, Jean Andrews, Kathy Matthews, Jean Bond-Slaughter

Production Staff: Richard L. Owsiany, Susan Dupere

Designer: Elizabeth Watson

Book Manufacturing: Lincoln & Allen Company

Printed in Hong Kong

Mention of the Pacific Northwest evokes powerful imagery, from the region's rugged ocean coast to massive mountain peaks, dense forests, and lush valleys, and to the rolling hills beyond. This topography along with dynamic Pacific weather patterns create the climate that, in turn, drives our seasonal rhythms—indeed, four distinct seasons. From the damp, mild coastal areas to the more extreme arid land east of the Cascade Mountains, the Northwest boasts a range of growing regions that yield a boggling array of foods. The Northwest—from Alaska and British Columbia to Washington, Idaho, Oregon, and Northern California—is a top national producer of apples, lentils, hops, hazelnuts, plums, peppermint, sweet onions, potatoes, and many types of berries. The ocean, bays, and rivers supply the region with a broad selection of fish and shellfish, and rain-soaked foothills give us prized wild mushrooms.

For the Northwest cook, this wealth of ingredients means ready access to mouth-watering edibles such as morels and asparagus with halibut in the spring, rich salmon with peaches and raspberries during summer, delicious pears, chanterelles, and cranberries harvested in the fall, and plump oysters and mussels in winter. The distinctive bounty of our regional foods makes for a culinary landscape that is as compelling as the natural landscape. This series of Northwest Homegrown Cookbooks shines the spotlight on those individual foods that flourish seasonally in this place that I call home. Savor this taste of the Northwest.

ACKNOWLEDGMENTS

Whole hosts of people helped make writing this book a wonderful adventure. First and foremost, thanks to my former boss, Peter Redmayne, with whom I worked while editor of *Simply Seafood* magazine. What an amazing training ground that was. I relish all that I learned during those years and the seafood expertise that Peter shares with me still. Jon Rowley is another longtime seafood guru who graciously allows me to pick his brain on matters of tasty things from the sea.

Many, many thanks to Harry Yoshimura and the whole crew at Mutual Fish in Seattle. Harry's knowledge of every ounce of seafood that passes through his doors makes him an outstanding resource for any seafood lover, writer or not.

Heather Reed and Richard Childers from the Washington Department of Fish & Wildlife, Gregory Jensen, a biologist with the University of Washington Department of Fisheries, David Gordon with the University of Washington Sea Grant, and Nick Furman, executive director of the Oregon Dungeness Crab Commission, were all exceptionally helpful with nitty-gritty details about our native crabs of the Northwest.

A number of foodie pals helped me discover the wonders of crab in their neck of the woods, including Bruce Aidells in San Francisco, and Sinclair Philip, Nathan Fong, and Kasey Wilson in British Columbia. Lane Hoss, marketing director for Anthony's restaurants, overwhelmed me with the spread of crab and selections of Northwest wines that she corralled for a unique crab wine-tasting experiment.

The idea for this series germinated a number of years ago in conversations with Marlene Blessing, then editor for Alaska Northwest Books®. Such a wealth of history, recipes, anecdotes, and personalities surround the iconic foods of this region. I'm thankful that Marlene was able to see the potential for books that shine the light one at a time on our key Northwest foods.

Thanks also to Kristine Britton for much-appreciated help with research, to ever-ready recipe testers Barbara Nims, Ed Silver, Michael Amend, Jeff Ashley, Tim and Katherine Kehrli, Joanne Koonce-Hamar, Charles and Rose Ann Finkel, and to the endless host of tasters who were willing to work for their supper, helping critique the recipes.

Finally, thanks to Don Barnett for the beautiful, vivid illustrations he has created for this book. And, as ever, to my husband, Bob, whose love and support is unending.

CONTENTS

Breakfast/Brunch 17

Appetizers 29

Soups and Sandwiches 45

Cooking with Crab 86

Introduction

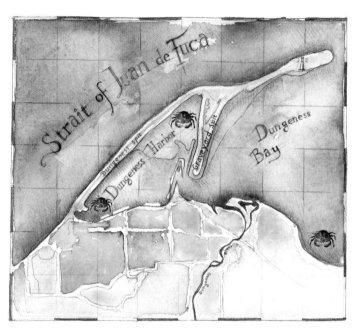

DUNGENESS SPIT, WASHINGTON STATE

When Captain George Vancouver explored the Strait of Juan de Fuca at the north edge of Washington State's Olympic Peninsula in the late eighteenth century, he happened upon a stretch of land that reminded him of a point on the English Channel called Dungeness. In dubbing this Washington spit the same, Vancouver inadvertently established the namesake for what would become one of the Northwest's most iconic foods.

The beautiful Dungeness crab, *Cancer magister,* was at first known simply as "edible crab" or just "crab." But as the fishery for this tasty, sweet crab became more significant in the early twentieth century, it took on the label "Dungeness." Today the Dungeness crab is one of the foods mostly closely identified with the Northwest.

From Alaska to central California, Dungeness is the crab you'll see piled high on ice at local markets and producing clouds of steam on the dinner table. But Northwest waters are home to dozens of other crab species, including tiny hermit crabs, yellow and purple shore crabs, odd-looking box crabs that seem excessively armored against their foes, and many rock crabs, the creatures we come upon when exploring the region's coastlines. This first volume in the Northwest Homegrown Cookbook Series focuses on the three species of crabs available commercially in the region: Dungeness crab, king crab, and, to a lesser degree, snow crab (also known as tanner crab).

When it comes to enjoying crab, simple is best for most seafood fanatics: freshly cooked crab, with melted butter and/or lemon wedges, plenty of napkins, and a crisp, cold beverage. From that simple starting point (see Northwest Crab Boil, page 66), this collection of more than forty regionally inspired recipes covers the gamut from Savory Crab Blintzes with Dill (page 22) to Crab and Tillamook Cheddar Sandwiches (page 55) to Rosemary Roasted Crab (page 85). Because Dungeness is by far the most commonly available crab in the Northwest, it is the crab I used for most of these recipes. A handful of the recipes start with whole crab to be cooked in-shell, but most rely on bulk crabmeat. For those recipes, you could use virtually any crabmeat: Dungeness, flaked king or snow, or even blue crabmeat if you happen to be cooking outside of the Northwest.

One of my favorite books in an eclectic collection is one of Seattle's first restaurant guides, *You Can't Eat Mount Rainier*. In that endearing book, writer Bill Speidel did what few locals were then willing to do: stand on a soapbox and exclaim loudly about the wonderful foods and great restaurants of the Northwest in the early 1950s. "Our greatest regional blessing, food fresh from the sea, is offered by our restaurants in bountiful array," writes Speidel. The first of these seafoods he mentions is "Dungeness crab, the most delicate, delightful crabmeat in the world."

A few decades later, Portland native James Beard echoed the sentiment in his classic cookbook, *American Cookery*: "There are many different crabmeats available throughout the country. . . . Having been brought up on Dungeness, I prefer it above other crabmeat." Like this noted gastronome, I too was brought up on Dungeness crab and consider it to be a taste of home.

Dungeness Crab

King Crab

Snow Crab

The Story of Northwest Crab

A Brief History

Of the dozens of crab species found in the waters of the Northwest, three contribute most to the commercial and culinary character of the Northwest: Dungeness, king, and snow crabs. The latter two are fished primarily in the deep, frigid waters of Alaska, while Dungeness are found from the Pribilof Islands of Alaska down to Santa Barbara, California.

The San Francisco Bay Area has the longest commercial history with Dungeness crab along the Pacific Coast. Early fishing records date back as far as 1848, when Italian settlers to the region began harvesting and selling local fish. This dawning industry grew quickly as the California gold rush gained steam, bringing new customers to the region as well as disillusioned prospectors who turned their attention from hopes of gold to heaps of seafood. It is believed that crab were initially an incidental catch—fishermen intending to catch anchovies, sole, or sardines would sometimes find crabs trapped in their nets. By the early 1860s, crabs were being marketed along the San Francisco waterfront and crabbing had become a more targeted fishery. Early crabbing records farther north on the Pacific Coast don't appear until near the end of the 1800s. Those early commercially harvested crab didn't make it far from the dock where they were landed, though, since there weren't yet systems in place to distribute the perishable shellfish.

It wasn't until the 1920s and '30s that a more significant crab fishery developed all up and down the coast, in tandem with advances in refrigeration and processing techniques as well as development of transportation networks. It was about this time, too, that the name "Dungeness" became attached to the distinctive reddish-purple crab so abundant here. Today the Washington coastal town of Sequim, which grew out of an early settlement on the Strait of Juan de Fuca, embraces the crustaceous critter that shares its name with the nearby Dungeness spit, historic Dungeness lighthouse, and the Dungeness River that spills out into Dungeness Bay. The Dungeness Golf & Country Club even boasts a crab-shaped sand trap on hole No. 3.

Species Information

While editor of *Simply Seafood* magazine, I had the rare treat of spending a week on Alaska's Kodiak Island, traditional home to not only the great brown bear (of which I got a surprisingly up-close view) but also to king crab. Back in the mid-1960s, Kodiak Island was Alaska's largest producer of king crab, landing nearly 91 million pounds in 1966. But stocks have declined significantly since peak harvests of Alaska king crab in the

1980s. Today there is no commercial king crabbing on Kodiak, but subsistence and sport crabbers on the island can still capture the tasty creatures. A most unforgettable feast during my visit to Kodiak was prepared by my hosts—seasonal salmon-fishing families from the Lower 48 as well as the locals from the village of Akhiok at the southern end of the island. The centerpiece in the midst of the salmon pirogs (pastry-topped savory pies), salmon quiche, and salmon pasta salads was a huge bowl of king crab legs which only hours earlier were still scurrying along the ocean floor. I'd been out in the skiff when the pots were brought up and was absolutely flabbergasted at the sight of those creatures, so big (they can grow as big as five feet or more from the tip of one leg to the other) and intimidating with their thorned shells.

Back on shore, a huge pot of seawater was brought to a boil over a propane burner while the crabs were cleaned. In no time we were all feasting on the incredible briny-sweet meat. It was enough to have me swearing off king crab enjoyed any other way (experiences like that are once in a lifetime, and rightfully so). That was until a more recent development that saw more and more king crab being transferred live to markets and restaurants in larger Northwest cities. Crabs are rather sturdy creatures and can survive a day or more out of water in the proper conditions. The king crab are put in large boxes and well chilled, which, in addition to preserving the quality of the meat, dulls their senses to keep them docile in transit. Upon arrival at their destination, generally less than 24 hours later, the crabs go into saltwater tanks and are fully revived. This is how I came to enjoy fresh king crab in a thoroughly urban setting—Vancouver, British Columbia's Sun Sui Wah Seafood Restaurant (see page 81).

In the years after World War II, crabbing for kings developed as an important fishery

Science Says: So, we know that crab is a gastronomic delicacy in the kitchen and on our dinner plates. But where does crab fit in the biologist's lab? First, crabs are part of a large group of creatures called arthropods—invertebrates with segmented bodies and jointed legs—which includes all insects, spiders, centipedes, and crustaceans (crabs, shrimp, lobsters, crayfish). Crabs are also classified as decapods, because they have ten legs. From this point the crab population falls into one of two groups: brachyurans and anomurans. The former are considered to be the "true" crabs because, true to decapods, they sport ten visible appendages: four pairs of legs and one pair of claws. Brachyurans include Dungeness, snow, rock, and purple shore crabs. The anomurans are also technically decapods, though only the claws and three pairs of walking legs are visible, the fourth set dwarfed and tucked under the back shell edge. Anomuran crabs in the Northwest include the glorious king crab, as well as an array of hermit crabs, box crab, and the wild-looking heart crab.

in Alaska. These deep-sea creatures thrive in the frigid waters of the North Pacific, and treacherous ocean conditions there have helped make king crab fishing among the most dangerous professions in the world. The fishery was abundant until the early 1980s, but the population of this prized crab has declined to such an extent that stiff limits were recently established to help allow the crab numbers to recover.

Red king crab (*Paralithodes camtschatica*) is the most abundant species of king crab, the iconic huge crab that's maroon-red when alive, turning bright orange-red when cooked. The size of red king crab generally ranges from four to ten pounds. Similar in size is the blue king crab (*Paralithodes platypus*), so named because of a slight bluish hue on the shells in its live state. When cooked, these blue kings turn the same fiery color as red king crab, and the two species are generally marketed as one. A smaller king specimen is the golden (or brown) king crab (*Lithodes aequispina*), which is fished in deeper waters of the North Pacific. This crab, too, is generally sold simply as "king," though the legs are more uniformly reddish-orange while the other kings have a pale creamy color on the underside of the legs.

Snow crab, the common name attached to tanner crab and opilio crab, is a much smaller crab than the king, averaging about two to four pounds. There are four species of snow crab in Alaskan waters, but only two—*Chionoecetes opilio* and *C. bairdi*—are fished commercially. Most snow crab comes from the Bering Sea and much of the catch goes to Japan. We don't see much snow crab in Northwest markets, likely because snow simply can't hold our attention when Dungeness is on the scene. And snow crab tends to be the one commonly offered at chain seafood restaurants and on surf 'n' turf menus around the country. Unless you get a rare opportunity to taste snow crab freshly cooked, it generally runs a distant third to king and Dungeness crabs in flavor and texture. It's easy to tell the difference between snow and king legs: king crab legs are round with sharp thorny bumps (be careful!) and snow crab legs, aside from being smaller, are flatter with smoother shells.

There's little doubt that the premier Northwest crab is the Dungeness. Even its Latin name, *Cancer magister,* is a clue to the regal status this creature holds. The fishery for Dungeness reaches from the Gulf of Alaska down the Pacific Coast to central California. Dungeness are caught as far south as Santa Barbara, though the major fishery in California is primarily from the San Francisco area north. From city-slicker seafood markets and restaurants to more rustic crab shacks along the coast, Dungeness is one of the most prized regional foods.

Seasonality

The commercial season for Dungeness crab is a long one, extending nearly year-round in various openings up and down the Pacific Coast. But December is when the big push hits, with the opening of the ocean fishery in many areas (typically on December 1). The bulk of the year's catch will come in the first month or two—and with high supply comes low prices, making it an ideal time to splurge on a big crab feed for family and friends. Through spring and summer as the fishery slows down, prices work their way up until most commercial crab fisheries close, generally in August or September.

Alaska's Dungeness season peaks during the summer, though depending on the level of landings, these crab may or may not have much impact on prices in the Lower 48. Fall's the annual low point, the time when the larger crabs are molting (smaller crabs molt a few times a year), shedding their undersized hard shell for a new, larger shell that will take about four to six weeks to harden. The launch of the commercial season in December is contingent on the majority of crabs having fully hardened shells, one key point that fisheries agents use for determining the opening date of the season.

In addition to this annual fluctuation of supply and prices, there is also a longer cycle that sees crab supplies rise and fall over an average of seven to ten years, though the pattern is anything but consistent. The year I was working on this book, for instance, the catch in Washington State was roughly seven million pounds, while for the preceding year crabbers in the state landed seventeen million pounds of Dungeness. There seems to be no single reason for this fluctuation, but influences can include climate, predators, oceanic conditions, and the crab's natural

tendency toward cannibalism. Given our modern food chain that's been well tailored to fit our love of consistent availability and prices, it can be frustrating to deal with the vagaries of nature for the supply of our favorite delicacies. But the best things in life—like crab at a price that has you calling friends over for a bountiful crab feed—are always worth waiting for.

True Northwesterners shrug at such market forces, jump in the car, and head to their favorite crabbing spot. (Sport season openings for Dungeness vary throughout the region and licenses are required—check with the Department of Fish and Game in your area.) One friend says that all he needs to stay stocked in Dungeness is "$1.49 worth of turkey meat for bait and some gas money," with his crab pot and car pointed in the general direction of Westport, Washington.

Sustainability is an ever-growing concern among the culinary and environmental watchdogs, but most agree that Dungeness crab is one of the most sustainable fisheries in the world. Only males of a certain size are harvested (both for commercial and recreational fishers) to ensure that they reach mating maturity at least one season prior to being caught. Each year roughly 90 percent of the legal-size male population is harvested. Not only are females left untouched to maintain a reproductive base, but they also do not reach the size of males and don't afford the same ratio and quality of meat.

About the Recipes

The bulk of the recipes in this book use Dungeness crab, simply because Dungeness is the premier Northwest crab—in quality and availability. By all means feel free to substitute other crab available to you. King and snow leg portions can be used in place of Dungeness portions where the crab is cooked in the shell. For recipes using bulk crabmeat, the meat from rock, stone, or blue crabs will generally be suitable substitutes. And some recipes offer a range in the amount of crab you could use, so you can embellish that Crab Louis more or less luxuriously according to your whim and budget.

It's tempting to believe that when you're using a recipe that calls for crabmeat, you'd save some money picking the meat yourself from a whole crab. But crab economics don't always work out that way. In a rough average, I found that the yield of meat from a whole cooked crab will be about 25 percent of the original weight, though it varies with the thoroughness of picking and with the crab itself—a larger crab will generally have a better meat-to-shell ratio than a smaller one. If your 2-pound crab costs you $5.50 per pound, that's $11. Since you'll get about ½ pound of meat from that crab, you're paying roughly $22 per pound for the meat itself. If the price for the bulk meat is in that price range, you'll save yourself plenty of time at little or no extra cost buying prepicked meat.

A Weighty Issue: While we American cooks are devoted to our measuring cups and spoons, much of the rest of the world uses more precise weight measures when cooking, and in some cases I do think it's a better system. The way you measure "1 cup crabmeat" may be different from the way that I do, depending on how much you pack the crab into the cup and if it's finely flaked or in bigger pieces. For this reason, I chose to use weight measure for recipes that use bulk meat. You can either purchase just the weight you need at the store, or consider getting yourself a kitchen scale. In a pinch, though, here are some rough cup-measure equivalents:

Crabmeat by weight and measurement

1 ounce = about 3 tablespoons	5½ ounces = about 1 cup	
2 ounces = about ⅓ cup	8 ounces = about 1½ cups	
4 ounces = about ¾ cup	1 pound = about 3 cups	

Breakfast / Brunch

Crab Benedict

Already an indulgence, with its blend of freshly poached eggs and rich hollandaise sauce, this breakfast classic is made even more special when plump, sweet crab replaces the traditional ham to serve as a bed for the eggs. It's a dish you'll see on breakfast menus across the Northwest and one I've had on more than a few occasions when visiting Westport, one of the busiest crabbing towns on the Washington coast. Because the crab-egg-hollandaise combination is so rich, I suggest just one muffin half per serving, but for heartier appetites you could serve two. Hash browns and/or fresh fruit would be a great finish.

This hollandaise sauce, traditionally flavored only with lemon juice, gets added flavor from a touch of lemon zest and orange zest, making the sauce a bit brighter in flavor. It is important to cook the hollandaise sauce over low heat so the egg yolks cook gently and thicken smoothly without becoming grainy. If your burner won't maintain low heat, cook the sauce in a bowl set over, but not touching, a pan of simmering water.

2 plain English muffins	4 eggs
4 ounces crabmeat	1 teaspoon minced chervil or chives
2 tablespoons distilled white vinegar	

Hollandaise Sauce

½ cup unsalted butter	½ teaspoon grated orange zest
2 tablespoons water	¼ teaspoon grated lemon zest
2 egg yolks	Salt and freshly ground white pepper
1 tablespoon freshly squeezed lemon juice	

For the hollandaise sauce, melt the butter in a small saucepan over medium-low heat. Using a small spoon, skim off and discard the milk solids that collect on the surface of the melted butter; set aside.

In another small saucepan, whisk together the water and egg yolks until blended. Set the saucepan over low heat and cook, whisking constantly, until the mixture has about doubled in volume and is frothy and thick, 5 to 7 minutes.

Take the pan from the heat and whisk in the melted butter in a thin, steady stream, leaving behind the milky sediment in the bottom of the pan. Whisk the lemon juice, orange zest, and lemon zest into the sauce, along with salt and pepper to taste. Keep the sauce warm over very low heat or over a pan of hot water.

Split and toast the English muffins and place them on a baking sheet. Pick over the crabmeat to remove any bits of shell or cartilage, and divide it evenly over the muffins. Keep the muffins warm in a low oven while poaching the eggs.

Half-fill a deep skillet with water and add the vinegar. Bring the water to a gentle boil over medium-high heat, then carefully crack the eggs into the water. (To avoid scalding your knuckles, you may first crack each egg into a small bowl, then gently tip the egg from the bowl into the water.) Reduce the heat to medium and simmer gently until the egg whites are set but the yolks are still soft, about 3 minutes, gently sloshing some of the water over the tops of the eggs once or twice during cooking to help set the surface of the yolks.

Scoop out the eggs with a slotted spoon, drain gently on paper towels, and set the eggs on the crab-topped muffins. Place each muffin on a warmed plate, spoon the hollandaise sauce over, and sprinkle with the chervil. Serve right away.

Makes 4 servings

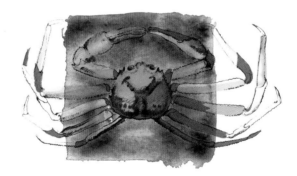

Fines Herbes Omelet with Crab

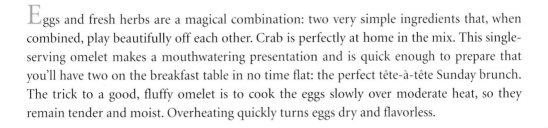

Eggs and fresh herbs are a magical combination: two very simple ingredients that, when combined, play beautifully off each other. Crab is perfectly at home in the mix. This single-serving omelet makes a mouthwatering presentation and is quick enough to prepare that you'll have two on the breakfast table in no time flat: the perfect tête-à-tête Sunday brunch. The trick to a good, fluffy omelet is to cook the eggs slowly over moderate heat, so they remain tender and moist. Overheating quickly turns eggs dry and flavorless.

For a change now and then, I like to serve a toasted baguette with my breakfast eggs: cut a baguette into roughly 5-inch lengths, and then cut each piece in half horizontally. Lightly toast the baguette under the broiler, then slather generously with butter.

2 eggs	¼ teaspoon minced flat-leaf
1 tablespoon water	(Italian) parsley
2 ounces crabmeat	⅛ teaspoon minced tarragon
1 tablespoon unsalted butter	Salt and freshly ground white or
½ teaspoon minced chives	black pepper
½ teaspoon minced chervil	Herb sprigs, for garnish (optional)

Crack the eggs into a medium bowl and beat with a fork until partially blended. Add the water and continue beating until the eggs are evenly blended and a little frothy. Pick over the crabmeat to remove any bits of shell or cartilage.

Melt the butter in a small skillet, preferably nonstick, over medium heat. Add the herbs to the eggs, along with salt and pepper to taste, and stir just to mix. Slowly pour the eggs into the skillet and cook until they are nearly set, 2 to 3 minutes. During this time, slowly draw a wooden spoon across the bottom of the pan in a spiral, starting at the outer edge and working your way to the center, then back out. Keeping the beaten eggs in motion helps assure that they cook evenly. When there is almost no liquid egg left, stop stirring, scatter the crabmeat evenly over the omelet, and cook until the omelet is set, 1 to 2 minutes longer.

Take the skillet from the heat. Using a heatproof spatula, fold one-third of the omelet toward the center, then fold that center portion again toward the opposite edge of the skillet. Carefully roll the omelet from the skillet onto a warmed serving plate. (Ideally, the "seam" will be on the bottom, though it doesn't really matter.) Serve right away, garnishing the plate with herb sprigs, if you like.

Makes 1 serving

Fines Herbes: *Fines herbes* is a French term for the combination of chervil, chives, parsley, and tarragon. Although the blend is commonly available in dried form, for this dish I highly recommend that you use fresh. Chervil is a delicate herb with lacy parsleylike leaves and a flavor reminiscent of anise. The herb can be hard to find fresh in markets but is easy to grow, so consider adding it to your kitchen garden or window box. You could use just chives and/or parsley if you prefer, about 1 teaspoon total. If you happen to have any chives blossoming in your garden, cut one on a long stem to lay over each omelet for a striking garnish.

Crab and Goat Cheese Breakfast Bruschetta

Slices of toasted rustic bread serve as an open-face foundation on which to layer goat cheese, crabmeat, and vine-ripe tomatoes—a tasty waker-upper. Mix and match other ingredients to suit your taste and the best of what's available at the market. Herbs added to the goat cheese could include chives, chervil, and tarragon (though not too much). When summer's tomatoes are no longer available, you could top the sandwiches with oven-roasted or sun-dried tomatoes, fresh leaves of baby spinach, or a few sprigs of parsley to add a bright finish. For a more substantial variation, scramble 4 or 5 eggs with the crab before piling it on the toast. Or simply serve scrambled eggs alongside the bruschetta.

4 slices country-style bread, about ¾ inch thick	Salt and freshly ground black pepper
8 ounces goat cheese	4 to 6 ounces crabmeat
1 tablespoon minced dill	1 large tomato, cored and cut into 8 thin slices

Preheat the broiler. Toast the bread slices on one side about 4 inches from the broiler element until lightly browned. Set aside on a wire rack to cool.

Crumble the goat cheese into a small bowl and mash it with a fork to soften it slightly. Add the dill with a pinch of salt and pepper and stir to mix well. Spread the goat cheese mixture over the untoasted side of the bread slices.

Pick over the crabmeat to remove any bits of shell or cartilage, and arrange the crab evenly over the goat cheese. Lay the tomato slices over the crab and serve.

Makes 4 servings

Savory Crab Blintzes with Dill

Blintzes are typically a sweet breakfast dish of crêpes with a mild cheese filling and fruit topping. In this savory twist, the crêpe batter contains fresh dill, adding flavor, aroma, and flecks of vibrant green to enclose the rich filling of ricotta with delicate crab. Add scrambled eggs and fresh orange slices alongside, and your day is off to a great start. If the blintzes are part of a larger brunch spread, you may want to serve just one per person rather than two.

1 container (15 ounces) part-skim
  ricotta cheese
½ cup small-curd cottage cheese
8 ounces crabmeat
2 tablespoons freshly squeezed
  lemon juice

2 tablespoons minced flat-leaf
  (Italian) parsley
1 teaspoon minced dill
½ teaspoon grated lemon zest
Salt and freshly ground black pepper
Sour cream, for garnish (optional)
Dill sprigs, for garnish

Crêpes

1 cup all-purpose flour
½ teaspoon salt
3 eggs
1¼ cups milk

2 tablespoons unsalted butter, melted
  and cooled, plus more for cooking
  the crêpes
2 teaspoons minced dill

For the crêpes, combine the flour and salt in a medium bowl and stir with a fork to mix, then make a well in the center. Break the eggs into a small bowl and beat with the fork just to mix. Add the milk and stir to blend. Pour the milk mixture into the well in the flour and begin incorporating the flour just until mixed. It's important not to overmix the batter or the crêpes will be tough rather than tender; it may be a bit lumpy, which is fine. Add the melted butter and dill and stir just to incorporate. Cover and refrigerate for 1 to 2 hours before cooking the crêpes.

Lightly coat an 8-inch crêpe pan or medium skillet with melted butter and heat it over medium heat. Stir the batter once again to remix it. Add a scant ¼ cup of the batter to the pan and quickly but gently swirl the pan so the batter evenly coats the base. Cook the crêpe until the surface turns from shiny to dull and the edges are just beginning to curl,

30 to 60 seconds. Using a small spatula, carefully flip the crêpe and cook on the second side until lightly browned on the bottom, about 1 minute longer.

Transfer the crêpe to a plate and continue with the remaining batter, stacking the crêpes one on top of the other. It's very common for the first (and sometimes second) crêpe to be a total failure, so don't think twice about tossing out early crêpes that don't work. You want a total of 8 good crêpes in the end.

Preheat the oven to 350°F. Lightly butter a 9-by-13-inch baking dish.

In a medium bowl, combine the ricotta and cottage cheeses and stir to blend. Pick over the crabmeat to remove any bits of shell or cartilage, and stir the crab into the cheese mixture. Add the lemon juice, parsley, dill, and lemon zest and stir to blend. Season the blintz filling to taste with salt and a hint of pepper.

Lay one crêpe on the work surface with the more attractive side down. Spoon a heaping ¼ cup of the blintz filling into the center of the crêpe and spread it out a bit to form a rectangle. Fold in the sides of the crêpe over the filling, then fold down the top edge, and finally fold the bottom edge up, making a tidy rectangular package.

Set the blintz, folded side down, in the baking dish, and repeat with the remaining crêpes and filling. Lightly brush the tops of the blintzes with more melted butter and bake until they are heated through, about 20 minutes.

Transfer the blintzes to individual plates, serving 2 per person. Garnish with a dollop of sour cream, if desired, and the dill sprigs, and serve right away.

Makes 4 servings

Crab and Artichoke Frittata with Fontina

I'm a bit of an artichoke purist and find that prepared artichokes, whether canned bottoms or bottled hearts, are always disappointing compared to their fresh counterparts. For that reason, this recipe starts with a couple of whole artichokes to be trimmed down to the bottoms and simmered. For a shortcut, you may certainly use canned artichoke bottoms; these tend to be smaller than what you'd get from a typical whole artichoke, so use twice as many. You may also use blanched asparagus in place of the artichokes, if you prefer.

I suggest below that a nonstick pan is preferable for this recipe, but I'm tempted to say that it is necessary. Eggs love to stick to a hot skillet, unless it is nonstick. If you have no other choice, consider using an extra tablespoon or two of butter.

1 lemon, halved (if using fresh artichokes)	8 ounces crabmeat
2 large artichokes or 4 canned artichoke bottoms	1 cup grated fontina or Swiss cheese (about 4 ounces)
2 tablespoons unsalted butter	8 eggs
½ cup thinly sliced red onion	Salt and freshly ground black pepper

If using fresh artichokes, fill a medium bowl with cold water and squeeze into it the juice from one lemon half, dropping the lemon half into the water as well. (If using canned artichoke bottoms, skip to preheating the oven.)

Using a small, sharp knife, cut the stem from one artichoke where it meets the base. With your fingers, pick off a few rows of the tough outer leaves (being careful to avoid their thorny tips) until you begin to see the bulbous outline of the artichoke bottom and the leaf bases are more pale than dark green. Using the knife, trim away the tough green skin covering the base and sides of the artichoke bottom. Rub the cut edge of the second lemon half over the artichoke to help avoid discoloration. Holding the remaining cone of leaves with one hand, cut away the leaves about ¼ inch above where they meet the artichoke bottom (the fuzzy choke will be removed after the bottoms are cooked). Put the artichoke bottom in the lemon water and repeat with the second artichoke.

Bring a medium pan of salted water to a boil over high heat. While the water is heating, cut a round of parchment or waxed paper to a circle about the same diameter as the pan. Add the artichoke bottoms, reduce the heat to medium, and lay the paper circle on the surface of the water. The paper helps keep the artichokes submerged so they won't discolor in contact with the air. Cook the artichokes until tender when pierced with the tip of a knife, 20 to 30 minutes, depending on their size. Drain the artichokes and run cold water over them to cool quickly; when cool enough to handle, scoop out the choke with a small spoon and discard it. Set the artichoke bottoms aside.

Preheat the oven to 375°F. Melt the butter in a medium ovenproof skillet, preferably nonstick, over medium heat. Add the onion and cook, stirring, until it just begins to soften, 3 to 5 minutes. Take the skillet from the heat and spread the onion out evenly over the bottom of the skillet. Cut the artichoke bottoms into ¼-inch slices and arrange them over the onion. Pick over the crabmeat to remove any bits of shell or cartilage, and scatter it over the vegetables, followed by the cheese.

Whisk the eggs in a medium bowl until well blended, then season to taste with salt and pepper. Pour the eggs gently over the frittata filling and return the skillet to medium heat until the bottom is set and the edges are beginning to firm up, 5 to 7 minutes. Transfer the skillet to the oven and bake just until the top is set and the eggs are cooked through, 5 to 7 minutes longer. Invert the frittata onto a serving plate, cut it into wedges, and serve right away.

Makes 6 to 8 servings

The Yoshimura Family's Mutual Fish

In today's modern business environment, we seldom hear much about multigenerational businesses—unless it's word of them closing. But in the Rainier Valley neighborhood of Seattle, Mutual Fish is a three-generation seafood shop that's going strong, well into its fifth decade of providing the city's home cooks and chefs with top-quality fish and shellfish.

Dick Yoshimura came to Seattle in his early teens and worked at seafood processors that used to line Seattle's waterfront, centered around the area where Colman Dock is today. In 1946, he bought the space vacated by the Old Main Fish Company at 14th and Yesler and opened Mutual Fish. Originally the retail store carried a wide variety of Japanese foods, catering to the neighborhood clientele. But over the years, seafood became increasingly a specialty of Mutual Fish—early on they even did custom canning in olive oil and smoking for their customers. It was in 1965 that Mutual Fish moved into a new space built at the current location on Rainier Avenue South, southeast of downtown Seattle. You'll still find moshi ice cream, wasabi-roasted peas, and fresh daikon radishes on racks alongside the live tanks full of Dungeness crab, oysters, clams, even abalone—but seafood is clearly what Mutual is all about. In fact, patriarch Dick Yoshimura worked with seafood experts at the University of Washington fisheries school in the early 1970s to develop what became the first live tanks for retail use in town.

Though Dick is still a daily presence at the store, his son Harry runs the show today, scrutinizing morning deliveries, overseeing wholesale accounts, and meeting with longtime customers to talk shop over coffee in the back room. Harry grew up with Mutual and is surely as at home here as anywhere. He remembers time spent on Lopez Island in the San Juans as a kid, pulling up crab pots, heating up seawater in a hug pot over a propane burner, boiling the crabs right there on the shore, and eating them right away. "Pretty dynamite," is how Harry remembers these feasts. It's a similar story heard by many a Northwesterner, whether they're reminiscing about their childhood summers so many years ago or that weekend on the coast last month. Mutual Fish is Seattle, it is the Northwest, and thankfully Harry's son Kevin too grew up with this store and is now very much part of the business. Seattleites and visitors alike can breathe a sigh of relief that Mutual Fish is sure to continue its long life in this seafood-loving city.

Crab and Leek Quiche

The simple quiche has been taken to some extremes over the years but remains at its best when eggs, cream, and cheese combine to cradle subtly flavored ingredients in a flaky crust. That's just what you'll find in this recipe: Gruyère is the cheese of choice (though Swiss is a nice alternative), with mildly oniony leeks embellishing the sweet crabmeat in the filling. This delicious quiche is an ideal option for breakfast, brunch, or lunch, or even as an appetizer.

2 tablespoons unsalted butter
2 large leeks, white and pale green
   parts only, split, cleaned,
   and thinly sliced
Salt and freshly ground black pepper

8 ounces crabmeat
1½ cups grated Gruyère cheese
   (about 5 ounces)
3 eggs
1½ cups half-and-half

Pastry Dough

1½ cups all-purpose flour
½ teaspoon salt
½ cup unsalted butter,
   cut into pieces and chilled

4 to 5 tablespoons ice water,
   more if needed

For the pastry dough, combine the flour and salt in a food processor and pulse once to mix. Add the butter pieces and pulse to finely chop the butter and create a mixture with a coarse, sandy texture. Drizzle the water into the dough, 1 tablespoon at a time, again pulsing briefly a few times just to blend in the water. It's important not to overmix the dough or it will be tough rather than flaky. The dough will not form a ball in the machine, but it has the proper amount of liquid if it feels neither dusty dry nor sticky when you squeeze some between your fingers. Turn the dough out onto the work surface, form it into a ball, and wrap it in plastic. Refrigerate the dough for at least 30 minutes before rolling it out.

While the dough is chilling, melt the butter in a small saucepan over medium heat. Add the leeks and cook, stirring occasionally, until just tender, about 5 minutes. Season lightly with salt and pepper and set aside to cool.

Preheat the oven to 400°F. Roll out the chilled dough on a lightly floured surface to a roughly 12-inch circle, and use it to line a 9- or 10-inch quiche or pie pan. Press the dough gently down the sides of the pan to be sure it is evenly covering the bottom. Using kitchen shears or a small knife, trim the outer edge of the dough to a ½-inch overhang, then fold that edge under and use your fingers to flute the pastry edge.

Prick the bottom of the shell with the tines of a fork, line the pastry shell with a piece of foil or parchment paper, and add pie weights or dry beans to cover the bottom. Bake the pastry shell until the edges are set, about 10 minutes. Take the pan from the oven, remove the foil and weights, and continue baking the crust until it is lightly browned and the bottom no longer looks raw, 3 to 5 minutes longer. (If the bottom of the shell starts to puff up, prick the dough again.) Take the crust from the oven and let cool slightly; reduce the oven temperature to 375°F.

Scatter the sautéed leeks over the bottom of the pastry shell. Pick over the crabmeat to remove any bits of shell or cartilage, and arrange it evenly over the leeks. Finally, sprinkle the Gruyère over the crab. In a medium bowl, whisk together the eggs to blend, then whisk in the half-and-half with a good pinch of salt and pepper. Pour the custard over the quiche filling. Bake the quiche until the top is lightly browned and a knife inserted in the center comes out clean, 30 to 40 minutes. (If the pastry edge browns too quickly, loosely cover it with a strip of foil to avoid burning.) Let it sit for about 5 minutes before cutting it into wedges to serve. The quiche can also be served at room temperature, though it needs to be refrigerated if you won't be eating it right away.

Makes 8 servings

Sourdough Bread Pudding with Crab

Bread pudding shows up in a lot of guises these days, from the traditional after-dinner sweet to savory side dishes that accompany roast meats. The classic dish moves to the breakfast table in this variation, with tangy sourdough bread enveloping sweet crabmeat in an herby custard.

1 small loaf day-old rustic sourdough
    bread (about 1 pound), cut into
    ½-inch cubes
2 cups grated cheddar cheese
    (about 8 ounces)
½ cup minced onion
12 ounces crabmeat

8 eggs
3 cups milk
2 tablespoons minced flat-leaf
    (Italian) parsley
1 tablespoon minced chives
Salt and freshly ground black pepper

Preheat the oven to 350°F. Generously butter a 9-by-13-inch baking dish.

Scatter about half of the bread cubes evenly over the bottom of the baking dish, and sprinkle all but ½ cup of the cheese over the bread, followed by the onion. Pick over the crabmeat to remove any bits of shell or cartilage, and scatter the crab over the onion, then top the crab with the remaining bread cubes.

In a medium bowl, whisk the eggs to blend, then whisk in the milk, parsley, and chives with salt and pepper to taste. Pour the egg mixture evenly over the bread and let sit for about 10 minutes, pressing the cubes down to help them evenly soak up the custard.

Sprinkle the reserved cheese over the top and bake the bread pudding until the top is lightly browned and a knife inserted in the center of the dish comes out clean, about 45 minutes. If the top is well browned before the eggy custard is cooked, loosely cover the dish with a piece of foil. Let the bread pudding sit for a few minutes before cutting it into pieces to serve.

Makes 8 servings

Appetizers

Fresh Spring Rolls with Crab and Hoisin Dipping Sauce

Fried spring rolls can be addictive for their crispness, but I prefer this nonfried version that allows the flavors of individual ingredients to shine more boldly. Fresh herbs and plump crab—with crunch from lettuce and body from cellophane noodles—make these simple spring rolls as easy to enjoy as they are to make. Rice paper wrappers come in brittle, semitranslucent rounds that need to be dampened before using. Look for them in Asian markets or on well-stocked grocery shelves near other Asian products.

1½ ounces cellophane
   (bean thread) noodles
8 round rice paper wrappers,
   8 inches in diameter
8 small green lettuce leaves, rinsed,
   dried, and halved (ribs discarded)

1 cup coarsely grated carrot
½ cup loosely packed mint leaves
½ cup loosely packed cilantro leaves
8 to 12 ounces crabmeat

Dipping Sauce

⅓ cup hoisin sauce
¼ cup dry vermouth
¼ cup water

½ teaspoon *sambal oelek* or other hot
   chile sauce, more to taste
¼ cup finely chopped roasted peanuts

Put the cellophane noodles in a small heatproof bowl and pour boiling water over them to cover. Let soak until tender, about 5 minutes, then drain well and let cool. When cool, cut the noodles into sections about 3 inches long using kitchen shears or a knife. Don't worry about the evenness of the pieces; you're just making the noodles easier to handle by portioning them a bit.

Lightly dampen a clean kitchen towel and lay it flat on your work surface. Fill a shallow dish, such as a pie pan, with hot tap water. Dip one of the rice paper wrappers in the water until evenly softened, 30 to 60 seconds, then transfer it to the towel and lay it out flat, patting the top lightly to remove excess water. Put another rice paper wrapper in the water to soften while you fill the first one.

Place a piece of lettuce on the lower half of the softened round. On top of the lettuce, arrange layers of about one-eighth each of the cellophane noodles, carrot, mint leaves, and cilantro leaves, then set the crabmeat on top. Fold the bottom quarter of the wrapper upward over the filling, then fold in each side and roll the package away from you to fully enclose the filling in a long cylinder. Repeat with the remaining wrappers and filling ingredients.

For the dipping sauce, combine the hoisin, vermouth, water, and chile sauce in a small bowl and stir to mix. For individual servings, provide a small dish or dipping sauce for each diner, or leave the sauce in a single bowl if serving from a platter. Sprinkle the peanuts over the sauce.

Cut each of the spring rolls in half crosswise, at a slight angle, and arrange the halves on individual plates or a platter. Serve right away, with the dipping sauce alongside.

Makes 4 to 8 servings

Crab and Avocado Tostadas

This variation on the familiar tostada makes great cocktail party fare. The tortilla pieces may be cut and toasted in the morning and then stored in an airtight container after they are fully cooled. Or, for a major shortcut, use good store-bought corn chips in place of the home-toasted tortillas, though the long, slender triangles used here make for a more elegant presentation and are sturdier than many commercial chips. The topping is best made not more than an hour before serving.

6 ounces crabmeat
1 ripe but firm avocado
3 tablespoons freshly squeezed
    lime juice
1 tablespoon minced cilantro
½ teaspoon minced jalapeño
Pinch ground cumin

Salt
6 corn tortillas
2 to 3 tablespoons vegetable oil
2 to 3 tablespoons sour cream
    (optional)
About ¼ cup loosely packed
    cilantro leaves

Pick over the crabmeat to remove any bits of shell or cartilage, and put it in a medium bowl. Peel and pit the avocado, cut it into small dice, and add it to the bowl. Drizzle the lime juice over the mixture, and use a fork to lightly mash the avocado while gently blending it with the crab. Add the minced cilantro, jalapeño, and cumin, with salt to taste. Stir gently to mix and refrigerate until ready to serve. The crab-avocado mixture should be a bit chunky rather than smooth.

Preheat the oven to 350°F. Lightly brush both sides of each tortilla with some of the oil. Cut each tortilla in half, then cut about ½ inch from the rounded edge opposite the diameter cut. (These trimmings can be discarded or toasted with the rest of the tortillas as a snack for the cook.) Halve the tortilla pieces diagonally to make 2 long, slender triangles, and lay the pieces on 2 baking sheets.

Toast the tortilla pieces in the oven until crisp and lightly browned, about 10 minutes, switching the baking sheets halfway through. Alternatively, you could toast the triangles on one sheet, half at a time. Let the tortilla pieces cool on a wire rack.

Just before serving, spoon a generous teaspoon of the crab-avocado mixture onto the broader end of each tortilla chip. Add a tiny dollop of sour cream (if using), and top with a cilantro leaf. Arrange the tostadas on a serving platter, and serve right away.

Makes 6 to 8 servings

Firecracker Crab Cocktail

This recipe is another example of simple being best: no lettuce, no filler, no frills, just crab and good homemade cocktail sauce. Although fresh horseradish makes a big difference, adding a fiery-hot kick to the sauce, prepared horseradish will give you respectable results as well. You could use ¾ cup of ketchup rather than both ketchup and chili sauce, though chili sauce does add a bit more texture to the mix.

I like to put a bit of the cocktail sauce in the dish first so that when you get to the bottom of your crab cocktail you still have some of the zesty sauce for the last of the crab. (It's the same philosophy I hold for hot fudge sundaes—it can be a drag to get to the bottom and realize there's no fudge sauce left!) For another presentation idea, consider big scallop shells commonly used for baked seafood dishes. Pile the crab in the center of a shell and spoon the cocktail sauce along one side, placing a wedge of lemon to the other.

12 to 16 ounces crabmeat   1 lemon, cut into wedges, for serving

Cocktail Sauce

½ cup ketchup
¼ cup chili sauce
2 tablespoons horseradish, preferably
   freshly grated

2 tablespoons freshly squeezed
   lemon juice
2 teaspoons minced green onion tops
½ teaspoon Worcestershire sauce
Hot pepper sauce to taste

For the cocktail sauce, combine the ketchup, chili sauce, horseradish, lemon juice, green onion, Worcestershire, and hot pepper sauce in a small bowl and stir to mix. Refrigerate until ready to serve. The sauce can be prepared up to a day in advance.

Just before serving, spoon about 1 tablespoon of the cocktail sauce into each of 4 small dishes. Pick over the crabmeat to remove any bits of shell or cartilage, and divide it among the dishes, reserving any whole leg pieces for the top. Spoon the rest of the cocktail sauce over the crab, set the dishes on small plates, and place the lemon wedges on the plates. Serve right away.

Makes 4 servings

The Crab Wine Experiment

Lane Hoss is the marketing director for Anthony's Restaurants, of which there are about twenty scattered around the Puget Sound region. Seafood is their claim to fame, and Sunday all-you-can-eat crab feeds are on the menu year-round at the seven HomePort restaurants. (Anthony's seafood buyer, Tim Ferleman, notes that in a busy week he can go through as much as 1,200 pounds of Dungeness crab.) But Lane's second love is wine, and her job description also includes overseeing the wine program at all the restaurants. Who better to help me understand the characteristics that help make a wine a good partner for crab.

When I showed up for our meeting at Anthony's Pier 66 on the Seattle waterfront one glorious summer afternoon, I saw twelve empty glasses on the table in front of me. And the chef was preparing four different crab dishes—cold steamed Dungeness, warm king crab legs, and crab cakes with two different sauces: beurre blanc and ginger plum—to taste with each of the wines. This was no simple chitchat about wine pairing, this was a full-on tasting experience. These observations, though, should be taken as such, food for thought rather than specific prescriptions for what wine to drink with what crab dish.

Here's what we learned:

- The plain steamed crab with no embellishment worked very well with bright, fruity wines such as pinot blanc, gewürztraminer, Johannisberg riesling, and chenin blanc; biggest faves in this category were Canoe Ridge Vineyard gewürztraminer from Walla Walla and pinot blanc from Willakenzie in the Willamette Valley. Typically, big chardonnays didn't taste right with this sweet, simple crab; one exception was a fruit-forward Hogue chardonnay that had much less oaky treatment than many other Northwest chardonnays.

- Crab cakes took the richness to another level and really changed the pairing field; the ginger-plum sauced cakes went better with those crisp, fruit-forward wines such as Hogue's chenin blanc, while bigger, oaky whites fought with the flavors from that sauce; the latter wines fared much better with the richness that the beurre blanc sauce brought to the pairing, so Chaleur Estate Blanc (a semillon–sauvignon blanc blend) from DeLille Cellars and Woodward Canyon's Celilo Vineyards chardonnay were good matches.

- King crab has much different character from Dungeness crab, so more full-flavored white wines found a better partnership here, particularly if the crab was dipped in melted butter; good matches here included L'Ecole No. 41 semillon and Chehalem pinot gris; on the flip side, some of those wines we loved with the plain Dungeness didn't taste nearly as good with the king, among them the Château Ste. Michelle Johannisburg riesling and Willakenzie's pinot blanc.

All but one wine we tasted were from Washington and Oregon. That welcome interloper? Veuve Cliquot Brut (nonvintage) champagne. The wine-savvy have known this for some time, but champagne makes a great food wine, not just for sipping before dinner. Every now and then through our experiment, a sip of Veuve perfectly balanced whatever level of sweetness or meatiness or brininess we were tasting at the moment.

Crab Pizza with Arugula and Fresh Mozzarella

This simple pizza recipe has no sauce to speak of, simply a brush of extra virgin olive oil over the dough before it is topped with crab and fresh mozzarella. The peppery crunch of arugula added just before serving makes a surprisingly delightful finish for the pizza. And I like the unexpected touch of heat from red pepper flakes too, though that's certainly optional. This small, thin-crusted pizza is meant to be served in wedges as a first course or snack, but it could also be served whole as a single main course serving.

Do seek out fresh mozzarella. Specialty markets and cheese shops are the best places to start, unless your neighborhood store is one of the gems that cares about top-quality cheese. You may use regular processed pizza-type mozzarella, though the rubbery texture and innocuous flavor bring much less to this recipe.

8 ounces crabmeat

4 ounces mozzarella, preferably fresh, cut into ¼-inch-thick slices

1 tablespoon fine cornmeal

2 tablespoons extra virgin olive oil

¼ teaspoon dried red pepper flakes (optional)

2 ounces arugula, rinsed, dried, and tough stems removed (about 1 cup, moderately packed)

Pizza Dough

1 cup all-purpose flour

½ teaspoon salt

⅓ cup warm water

1 teaspoon dry yeast

1 tablespoon olive oil

For the pizza dough, put the flour in a small bowl, making a well in the center. Along the outer edge of the well, make a small indentation in the flour and put the salt into that pocket (it shouldn't come in contact with the yeast while it's proofing). Pour the warm water directly into the well and sprinkle the yeast over the water. Set aside to allow the yeast to activate, about 5 minutes. Stir the dough, gently drawing in the flour from the edges and sprinkling with the olive oil as you go. When the dough becomes cohesive and forms a ball, transfer it to a lightly floured work surface and knead until it becomes smooth and satiny, about 10 minutes.

Put the dough in a lightly oiled bowl (it can be the same bowl you mixed the dough in), and turn it to evenly but lightly coat the dough with oil. Cover the bowl with a clean kitchen towel and set aside in a warm place until the dough has risen by about half, about 1½ hours.

Preheat the oven to 400°F. (If using a pizza stone, follow the manufacturer's instructions, which generally call for preheating the stone with the oven.) Pick over the crabmeat to remove any bits of shell or cartilage, and lay it on a double layer of paper towel to drain; also drain the mozzarella slices on paper towels, if using fresh cheese. Drawing off excess moisture from the crab and cheese will help ensure that the pizza doesn't get soggy.

Turn the risen dough out onto a lightly floured work surface and knead it gently. Press the dough out into a rough circle and roll it out to about 12 inches across. The dough will resist being rolled out and will insist on springing inward after a few swipes of the rolling pin. When this happens, let the dough rest for a minute or two before continuing.

If using a pizza stone that is preheated in the oven, sprinkle the cornmeal on a pizza peel or on an upside-down baking sheet, and lay the dough on top. Otherwise, simply sprinkle the cornmeal on a heavy baking sheet and top with the dough. Brush about 1 tablespoon of the olive oil over the dough, leaving a 1-inch perimeter that is not oiled. Scatter the crabmeat evenly over the oiled dough and lay the cheese slices over the crab, in a random pattern. Sprinkle with the pepper flakes, if using.

For the pizza stone bakers, slide the pizza carefully but quickly from the baking sheet onto the preheated stone (your instruction booklet should have pointers on this trick). Otherwise, simply put the baking sheet in the oven and, either way, bake until the crust is really crisp and the cheese is gently melted, 12 to 18 minutes. Take the pizza from the oven and scatter the arugula leaves evenly on top. Drizzle the remaining tablespoon of olive oil over the arugula, cut the pizza into wedges, and serve.

Makes 4 servings

Crab and Corn Soufflé

Don't be intimidated by the idea of making a soufflé. It's much easier than you may think, and there's nothing quite so impressive as a soufflé fresh from the oven, all puffed and golden, to start a meal with style. The simple combination of flavors from the corn and crab is quite wonderful, but if you'd like to add herbs, feel free. I'd suggest a tablespoon or two of minced chives, chervil, or parsley. This soufflé could also be served as a light main course.

For the best results, follow the technique described below for scraping the tender meat from the corn kernels, leaving as many of the tough skins behind on the ear as possible. This technique assures tender, moist corn that blends well with the soufflé base without weighing it down. It's kind of messy, though, so have a good section of counter cleared, to make it easier to collect stray corn. You can instead just cut the whole kernels from the ear (if you do, you won't need all of both ears to get the 1 cup needed) and chop them finely before continuing, though the resulting soufflé won't be as delicate.

Dry bread crumbs, for coating soufflé dish

6 ounces crabmeat

2 ears tender sweet corn, husks and silk removed

3 tablespoons unsalted butter

¼ cup all-purpose flour

1 cup half-and-half

1½ teaspoons Dijon mustard

½ teaspoon salt

¼ teaspoon freshly ground white or black pepper

¼ cup minced green onion

2 egg yolks

4 egg whites

Preheat the oven to 350°F. Generously butter a 1½-quart soufflé dish and coat it with dry bread crumbs, tapping the dish gently to remove the excess. Pick over the crabmeat to remove any bits of shell or cartilage, and break up any large pieces.

Using the tip of a sharp knife, carefully split each row of corn kernels from one end of the ear to the other. Holding the ear upright on the work surface, run the back of the knife down the ear to remove the tender meat of the corn, leaving as much of the tough kernel skin behind as possible. Transfer the corn pulp (you should have about 1 cup) to a bowl and set aside.

Melt the butter in a medium saucepan over medium heat. Add the flour and cook until it foams, stirring often with a whisk, about 3 minutes. Slowly add the half-and-half and whisk to mix well. Cook until thickened, 3 to 5 minutes longer. Whisk in the mustard, salt, and pepper. Take the pan from the heat and whisk in the crabmeat, corn, green onion, and egg yolks. Set aside. (The soufflé base can be made a few hours ahead and refrigerated, but let it sit at room temperature for a bit to take the chill off before continuing.)

Beat the egg whites until stiff; do not overbeat or they will become grainy. Add one fourth of the egg whites to the crab mixture and stir to lighten the soufflé base. Gently fold in about half the remaining egg whites, then fold in the last of the egg whites until thoroughly combined.

Pour the soufflé mixture into the prepared dish, smoothing the top. Bake until it is puffed up tall and nicely browned on top, 35 to 40 minutes. Serve immediately.

Makes 4 to 6 servings

Crab Cornmeal Fritters with Lime Aïoli

These fritters may hint at hush puppies—traditionally Southern fare—but the nuttiness of cornmeal is a nice complement for crabmeat, and the combination is particularly well suited to deep-frying. The citrus tang of the lime aïoli is a tasty contrast to the rich fritters.

Temperature control when deep-frying is important, not only for your safety but to assure that the fritters will be cooked through, not still gooey, when the outside is nicely browned. It's best to use a cooking thermometer to keep tabs on the oil temperature while you're frying.

6 ounces crabmeat
Vegetable oil, for frying
½ cup cornmeal
¼ cup all-purpose flour
1½ teaspoons baking powder
¼ teaspoon salt

⅛ teaspoon freshly ground
   black pepper
¼ cup milk
1 egg, lightly beaten
1 teaspoon grated lime zest
Lime wedges, for serving

Lime Aïoli

1 egg yolk
1 tablespoon freshly squeezed lime juice
2 cloves garlic, finely chopped

¾ cup olive oil (not extra virgin)
½ teaspoon grated lime zest
Salt and freshly ground white pepper

For the lime aïoli, combine the egg yolk, lime juice, and garlic in a food processor and pulse to blend. With the motor running, begin adding the oil, a drop or two at a time, until the yolk mixture starts to thicken, showing that an emulsion is beginning to form. Continue adding the oil in a thin, steady stream. When all the oil has been added, add the lime zest, with salt and pepper to taste, and pulse a few more times to mix evenly. Transfer the aïoli to a bowl, cover with plastic wrap, and refrigerate until ready to serve. The aïoli will have a more pronounced flavor if made a couple hours before serving.

Pick over the crabmeat to remove any bits of shell or cartilage, flaking up any large pieces of crab and squeezing the meat in your fist to remove excess liquid; set aside.

Heat about 3 inches of oil in a large, heavy saucepan (the oil should not come more than halfway up the sides of the pan) over medium-high heat to about 375°F. While the oil is heating, combine the cornmeal, flour, baking powder, salt, and pepper in a medium bowl and stir to mix. Add the milk and egg and stir to make a smooth, thick batter. Add the crab to the batter with the lime zest and stir to blend evenly.

When the oil is hot enough, scoop up a tablespoonful of the fritter batter and use another spoon to help drop it gently into the hot oil. Cook 4 or 5 fritters at a time until they are nicely browned and cooked through, carefully turning them once or twice so they cook evenly, 4 to 5 minutes. Scoop out the fritters with a slotted spoon and drain on paper towels. Keep the fritters warm in a low oven while cooking the rest of the batter, allowing the oil to reheat as necessary between batches.

Arrange the hot fritters on individual plates, spoon some of the lime aïoli alongside, and add a lime wedge to each plate. Serve right away, passing the rest of the aïoli separately.

Makes 4 to 6 servings

Phyllo Tartlets with Curried Crab

Curry isn't among the seasonings commonly associated with the Northwest, but its deeply aromatic, warming character is certainly welcome here. We have Trader Vic's restaurants to thank for helping bring the exotic flavors of the Pacific Islands and beyond to the West Coast during the white-bread era of the mid-20th century. This appetizer is in honor of that colorful character, restaurateur Victor "Trader Vic" Bergeron. I can still remember what an adventure it was to eat at his Seattle restaurant, long closed but once the place to be in the Westin Hotel (originally the Washington Plaza Hotel) downtown.

16 sheets phyllo dough, thawed if frozen	6 ounces crabmeat
½ cup unsalted butter, melted	2 eggs
1 tablespoon unsalted butter	¾ cup unsweetened coconut milk
⅓ cup minced green onion	1 tablespoon dry sherry
1 tablespoon curry powder	Salt and freshly ground black pepper

Preheat the oven to 375°F. Lightly butter a 12-cup muffin tin.

Lay 1 sheet of phyllo dough on a work surface and lightly but evenly brush it with melted butter. Top with another sheet of dough, matching the sides up as evenly as possible. Brush with more butter and continue layering until you have used 8 sheets. Trim 1 inch from each edge of the phyllo stack and discard the trimmings. Cut the dough in half lengthwise, then across in thirds to make 6 squares (each about 5 inches square). Repeat with the remaining 8 sheets of dough.

Line the muffin tins with the pastry squares, pressing the bottom down gently to make a flat base. Use kitchen shears to round off the corners a bit, which tend to brown too much while baking. Cover the pan with a kitchen towel to keep the phyllo from drying out while you make the filling.

Melt the 1 tablespoon butter in a small skillet over medium heat. Add the green onion and cook, stirring, until softened and aromatic but not browned, 2 to 3 minutes. Add the curry powder and stir to mix, cooking for about 1 minute longer. Take the skillet from the heat. Pick over the crabmeat to remove any bits of shell or cartilage, and stir the crabmeat into the curry mixture until evenly blended with the seasoning; set aside to cool slightly.

Divide the crab mixture evenly among the phyllo shells. Lightly beat the eggs in a medium bowl, and then whisk in the coconut milk and sherry, with salt and pepper to taste. Ladle the custard mixture into the phyllo shells, pressing down on the crab to ensure that it's submerged under the custard. Bake until the custard is set and the phyllo is browned, 15 to 20 minutes. Let cool in the tin for a few minutes, then carefully remove the tartlets and arrange them on a serving platter. Serve right away.

Makes 6 servings

Sushi Roll with Crab and Daikon Sprouts

I'm a strong believer in going to the sushi bar and watching all the action—that, after all, is half the fun of having sushi—but there's also something to be said for staying home and making it just the way you like it. This is a great recipe for king or snow crab leg meat, if available, though you could use Dungeness crab (preferably leg pieces) as well. Here peppery daikon-radish sprouts and rich avocado are teamed with the crab. You may vary the combination to suit your taste, using julienned cucumber or radish, for example.

Many of these ingredients—nori (deep green dried-seaweed sheets), pickled ginger, daikon-radish sprouts, and wasabi—are not generally available in traditional grocery stores. You may need to make a special trip to a good Japanese market or a well-stocked grocery store, but the effort will pay off. Wasabi is most commonly sold in powdered form (just add water). Northwest wasabi growers make fresh wasabi an option local cooks didn't have in years past (see below), although availability is rather hit-and-miss. Look for it in specialty Asian markets or high-end grocery stores.

The body and stickiness needed for sushi rice comes from short-grain rice, which has a higher starch content than long-grain rice. Tobiko is flying fish roe, the tiny, firm fish eggs that serve as common garnish for sushi; the roe is often available in vibrant orange, though you may also find a pale green wasabi-infused version of tobiko as well.

8 ounces crabmeat	2 ounces daikon radish sprouts
4 sheets nori, 8 by 7 inches	½ ripe but firm avocado
1 ounce tobiko roe	Wasabi, pickled ginger, and soy sauce

Sushi Rice

2 cups short-grain rice	1 tablespoon sugar
2 cups water	1½ teaspoons salt
¼ cup seasoned rice vinegar	

For the sushi rice, put the rice in a sieve and run cold water over it, gently shaking the sieve, until the water draining from the bottom runs clear. Drain the rinsed rice well,

Fresh Wasabi: Most of us know the wasabi that starts in tins as a green powder: just add water and you've got the green paste so commonly served with sushi. This ubiquitous condiment does have a fresh form, however, and Northwest producers (particularly Pacific Farms in Florence, Oregon) are responsible for a resurgence of fresh wasabi that's available in markets and restaurants throughout the region.

Technically a rhizome, the rootlike fresh wasabi bulb has a fresh, peppery flavor that's very different from the powdered form. It is typically grated on a rough, pointed surface like that of a ginger grater, making a coarse paste. You can also grate it on a more traditional grater, but use the smallest grating holes possible. As distribution of fresh wasabi bulbs increases, more and more Japanese restaurants and specialty markets (such as Uwajimaya) are carrying it. Don't flip out over the per-pound price (which might be as much as $60!): one piece will cost only $5 or so and is plenty for a generous mound of this freshly grated treat. Also, you can purchase fresh wasabi by way of Pacific Farms' website, www.freshwasabi.com.

then put it in a small saucepan with the water. Cover the pan and bring the water just to a boil over medium-high heat. Immediately reduce the heat to low and cook until the liquid is fully absorbed, about 15 minutes. Take the pan from the heat and set aside, covered, for another 10 minutes.

While the rice is sitting, combine the vinegar, sugar, and salt in a small saucepan and heat gently just until the sugar and salt are dissolved; set aside.

Transfer the rice to a wooden bowl, if possible, or to a shallow dish such as a 9-by-13-inch baking dish. Spread the rice out with a large wooden spoon and drizzle the vinegar mixture evenly over it. Stir the rice to coat all the grains evenly with the vinegar mixture, making sure to draw rice in from the corners and edges; continue stirring until the rice cools to room temperature. It's important to not let the rice sit while still warm or the grains will meld together and the rice will be much harder to work with. The traditional method calls for fanning the rice while stirring to help it cool faster; if you have an extra pair of hands in the kitchen, you might ask for some help.

Once the rice has cooled, cover it with a slightly dampened paper towel and set aside. (Do not refrigerate the rice; it should be used within a couple hours of being made.)

If using crab leg pieces that are more than ½ inch thick, cut them in half lengthwise; if using bulk crabmeat, pick over it to remove any bits of shell or cartilage.

Lay 1 sheet of nori on a work surface, with the longer edge facing you. Top the nori with one-fourth of the sushi rice, pressing it out in an even layer with the back of a spoon (leaving a 1-inch border along the far edge). Spoon one-fourth of the tobiko horizontally across the center of the rice, and top it with one-fourth of the daikon sprouts, allowing some of the top sprout tufts to hang just over each end of the nori sheet. Peel the avocado half, cut it into quarters, and cut one of those quarters into a few slices. Lay those slices over the sprouts, and top the avocado with one-fourth of the crabmeat.

Roll up the bottom edge of the nori over the filling and continue rolling away from you, forming a tight cylinder. Set the roll aside, seam down, and repeat with the remaining ingredients.

When all the rolls are formed, cut each one across into 8 slices and arrange them on a serving platter or individual plates. Set a small mound of wasabi and a pile of pickled ginger alongside, passing soy sauce separately for each guest to use to taste (providing each with a small dish for the soy sauce, if possible).

Makes 6 to 8 servings

Sherried Crab and Mushrooms on Toast

This dish is simple comfort food at its best, a recipe that can be dressed up for a fancy dinner party (serve with a small mesclun salad, tossed with a sherry vinaigrette) or dressed down for a quick midnight snack (forget trimming the bread, just serve the creamy crab mixture on a piece of toast fresh from the toaster). To garnish this retro recipe in 1950s style, you could scatter some chopped hard-cooked egg on top just before serving.

2 tablespoons unsalted butter
1 cup thinly sliced mushrooms
½ cup finely chopped onion
2 tablespoons all-purpose flour
1½ cups half-and-half
8 ounces crabmeat

3 tablespoons dry sherry
Salt and freshly ground black pepper
6 slices white bread,
   crusts trimmed
2 tablespoons minced flat-leaf
   (Italian) parsley

Melt 1 tablespoon of the butter in a medium skillet over medium heat. Add the mushrooms and onion and sauté until tender, about 5 minutes. Sprinkle the flour over the vegetables and stir until they are evenly coated; then pour in the half-and-half. Cook, stirring often, until the sauce is thickened and well blended, 5 to 7 minutes.

Pick over the crabmeat to remove any bits of shell or cartilage, and add it to the sauce with the sherry. Reduce the heat to medium-low and cook just until the crab is heated through, 2 to 3 minutes. Season the sauce to taste with salt and pepper.

Toast the bread and cut each piece in half diagonally, forming 2 triangles. Butter the toast lightly with the remaining 1 tablespoon butter, and lay 2 triangles, slightly overlapping, in the center of each of 6 warmed small plates. Spoon the sherried crab mixture over the toast, sprinkle the parsley over the crab, and serve right away.

Makes 6 servings

Soups and Sandwiches

Spring Pea Soup with Crab Mousse

This vibrant green pea soup is distinctively accented with a delicate crab mousse that is subtly flavored with fresh mint. If you're using shell peas, the general rule of thumb is that 1 pound in the pod will produce 1 cup shelled peas, so you'll need 4 pounds of in-shell peas. If using frozen peas, be sure to look for the "petite" variety, which tends to be more tender and flavorful than regular frozen peas.

2 tablespoons unsalted butter
1 cup chopped onion
4 cups freshly shelled English peas or
    frozen petite peas (about 1 pound)

4 cups vegetable stock or chicken stock,
    preferably unsalted
½ cup whipping cream or half-and-half
2 teaspoons minced mint
4 mint leaves, for garnish

Crab Mousse

5 ounces crabmeat
1 whole egg
1 egg white

2 tablespoons whipping cream
1½ teaspoons minced mint
Salt and freshly ground white pepper

For the mousse, pick over the crabmeat to remove any bits of shell or cartilage, and squeeze the meat gently in your fist to remove excess water. Put the crab in a food processor and pulse a few times to chop it up a bit, and then add the whole egg and egg white and pulse to form a smooth purée, scraping down the sides a few times to ensure that the ingredients are well mixed. Add the cream and pulse to mix. Transfer the purée to a small bowl and stir in the mint with a pinch of salt and pepper. Refrigerate the mixture for about 1 hour.

Preheat the oven to 350°F. Lightly butter four ¼-cup ramekins or other small ovenproof dishes (you can use larger ramekins, though the mousse will be shallower and will need a bit less cooking time). Spoon the crab mousse mixture into the ramekins and set them in a baking dish. Add boiling water to the baking dish to come about halfway up the sides of the ramekins. Bake the mousse until it is lightly browned on top, pulls away from the sides of the ramekins, and is firm to touch, 20 to 25 minutes.

While the mousse is baking, prepare the soup. Heat the butter in a medium saucepan over medium heat. Add the onion and cook, stirring, until tender and aromatic,

3 to 5 minutes. Stir in the peas, and then add the stock. Bring the liquid just to a boil, reduce the heat to medium-low, and simmer for 10 minutes.

Purée the soup with an immersion blender or in batches in a food processor or blender. Pass the soup through a sieve, pressing on the solids with a rubber spatula to remove as much of the liquid and purée as possible, leaving only the tough skins. Scrape the purée clinging to the bottom of the sieve into the soup. Return the soup to the saucepan, stir in the cream and mint, and season the soup with salt and pepper. Gently reheat the soup over medium heat.

When the mousse is cooked through, carefully lift the ramekins from the baking dish and unmold the mousses upside down onto a plate. Ladle the soup into 4 warmed shallow soup bowls, set a mousse in the center of each bowl, and garnish the mousse with a mint leaf. Serve right away.

Makes 4 servings

Chilled Tomato Soup with Crab

A handful of sweet crabmeat is an ideal foil for the zesty, fresh flavors of the vegetables in this gazpacho-like soup. There is no replacement for the flavor and texture of summer's fresh tomatoes—though really good, ripe hothouse tomatoes are the next best thing. Likewise, fresh corn that's still tender and sweet, not starchy, is the best choice. This soup is the essence of summer in a bowl.

3½ cups tomato juice, regular or spicy

1 ear tender sweet corn (white or yellow), husk and silk removed

2 pounds vine-ripe tomatoes, cored, seeds removed, and coarsely chopped

1 large cucumber, peeled, seeded, and coarsely chopped

1 large red bell pepper, cored, seeded, and coarsely chopped

1 cup chopped red onion

½ cup loosely packed flat-leaf (Italian) parsley leaves

¼ cup loosely packed cilantro leaves

3 tablespoons olive oil

2 cloves garlic, finely chopped

Hot pepper sauce (optional)

Salt and freshly ground black pepper

8 to 12 ounces crabmeat

Pour about ½ cup of the tomato juice into an ice cube tray to make 6 cubes, and freeze until solid.

Trim the stem end of the ear of corn and set the ear upright on a cutting board. Use a sharp knife to cut away a few rows of the kernels at a time, turning the ear until you have cut away all of the kernels. Bring a small saucepan of salted water to a boil, add the corn kernels, and cook for 1 minute. Drain the corn, run cold water over it to cool, and drain well; refrigerate until ready to serve.

Put half of the tomatoes, cucumber, bell pepper, and onion in a food processor and pulse until finely chopped. Do not thoroughly purée them; you want to keep some texture and crunch. Transfer the mixture to a large bowl and repeat with the remaining vegetables, adding the parsley, cilantro, olive oil, and garlic to this batch. Stir this mixture into the bowl along with the remaining 3 cups tomato juice. (Alternatively, you can prepare the soup in a blender, chopping the vegetables in 4 or 5 batches.) Season the soup to taste with hot pepper sauce, salt, and pepper, and refrigerate until ready to serve, at least 1 hour.

To serve, ladle the soup into chilled soup bowls and sprinkle with the corn kernels. Pick over the crabmeat to remove any bits of shell or cartilage, and arrange it in a small pile in the center of each bowl. Add one tomato ice cube to each bowl, passing hot pepper sauce separately. Serve right away.

Makes 6 servings

Whiskey Crab Soup

This recipe was created in honor of Whiskey Flats at Dungeness Spit, the tidal flats at the Dungeness River delta below the bluffs where the area was first settled. The name is derived from an entrepreneurial spirit who sold bootleg whiskey there. The bisque-style soup is enriched with cream and finished with a scatter of chives for a fresh, lively accent.

Some better grocery stores and specialty food markets may have good fish stock in the freezer section—check the label to see whether it is concentrated, and dilute as instructed before using. Otherwise, fish stock is easy to make at home. Consider making a double batch and freezing the rest, an easy shortcut for your next chowder or fish stew. You could also use a low-salt chicken stock in its place.

2 tablespoons unsalted butter
1 cup finely chopped onion
3 tablespoons all-purpose flour
4 cups fish stock
8 ounces crabmeat

2 cups half-and-half or whipping cream
¼ cup whiskey, plus more for serving
    if desired
Salt and freshly ground white pepper
2 teaspoons chopped chives

Melt the butter in a medium saucepan over medium heat. Add the onion and cook, stirring occasionally, until tender and aromatic, 3 to 5 minutes (the onion should soften but not brown). Sprinkle the flour over the onion and continue cooking, stirring until evenly coated. Slowly pour in the fish stock and bring just to a boil, stirring often. Reduce the heat to medium-low and simmer, stirring until the soup is slightly thickened, 5 to 7 minutes.

Pick over the crabmeat to remove any bits of shell or cartilage, and add it to the soup with the half-and-half and whiskey, stirring to blend. Simmer just until the soup is heated through, about 5 minutes. Season the soup to taste with salt and pepper, and ladle it into individual warmed bowls. Scatter the chives over the soup and serve, passing a small pitcher of extra whiskey at the table, for diners to add a final splash to taste if they like.

Makes 4 to 6 servings

Fish Stock

Ask at your local fish market or counter for clean, white fish bones. If none are available, stock can be made with inexpensive fillet pieces. Halibut, cod, sole, and rockfish are good stock options; stronger fish such as salmon or Chilean sea bass are not good candidates for the stockpot. The fillets will release most of their flavor to the liquid, so are not much worth keeping after straining from the stock.

2 pounds fish bones, or 1½ pounds fish fillets, cut into pieces	2 or 3 sprigs thyme
½ cup coarsely chopped onion	1 bay leaf
2 stalks celery with leaves, sliced	8 to 10 whole black peppercorns

Rinse the fish bones or fillet pieces thoroughly in cold water and drain.

In a large saucepan, combine the fish bones or fillet pieces, onion, celery, thyme, bay leaf, and peppercorns. Add enough cold water to cover the ingredients by about an inch. Bring the water just to a boil over medium-high heat, reduce the heat to medium-low, and simmer, uncovered, for 20 minutes (counting from the time that the water boils). Use a large spoon to skim off any scum that rises to the top as the stock simmers, to help keep it clear.

Line a fine-mesh sieve with a dampened paper towel and place it over a large bowl. Take the stock from the heat, pour it carefully through the sieve, and let drain. Discard the bones or fillet pieces and vegetables and set the stock aside to cool. Any extra stock can be frozen for 2 to 3 months.

Makes about 1½ quarts

A Crab Feast without Parallel

I figured that during a visit to Vancouver Island's Sooke Harbour House to meet and talk crab with owner Sinclair Philip, my dinner might include some of the delectable crustacean. In fact, throughout the dining room—on the shelves of an old bookcase and hanging from most of the walls—I saw perfect, beautiful shells of crabs of all types collected from the waters around the exquisite inn. Some were clearly Dungeness, others odd-looking creatures with long spindly legs or heavy, spiked shells. The collection only hints at the wide variety of crabs available in the Northwest, including Sooke Harbour and the Strait of Juan de Fuca, over which the inn's twenty-eight guestrooms look.

I wasn't quite prepared for the feast that chef de cuisine Edward Tuson had in store for me. It was six courses of crab delights, a meal that perfectly exemplified the culinary consciousness that has earned Sooke Harbour House accolades as one of the top restaurants in North America. One thing about dining at Sooke, you are feasting on your surroundings, quite literally: herbs, flowers, vegetables, and greens come from the garden just outside the dining room windows; meat, cheeses, and other provisions from producers on Vancouver Island; and the seafood from the waters near the inn.

The first plate arrived with a distinct waft of fresh briny-ocean aroma, as if I were sitting at the tideline on the water's edge below us. Such multisensory delights continued throughout the meal. Here are a few of my crab-feast highlights:

- a tower layering crabmeat with cured salmon, pickled turnip, mustard leaves, and mint, the tall cylinder wrapped in a crisp, delicate sheet of fried sea lettuce, a variety of seaweed; a tuberous begonia flower adorned the top of the tower.

- an ethereal savory egg custard with crab, tiny smoked oysters, and nasturtium flowers, topped with a small fritter of crab blended with salicornia (also known as samphire or sea beans).

- a unique take on sushi, replacing the rice with barley, embellished with tulip, pickled sea lettuce, and crab; garnishing the plate was a most extraordinary surprise: beautiful red and white tulip petals held crisp flakes of crab that had been dried overnight in a low oven.

- a crab "bombe" that began with little purple shore crabs cooked up with aromatic vegetables and puréed to make a base to which crabmeat, butter, and agar-agar (a seaweed-based gelatin-like product) were added, seasoned with sweet cicely and other herbs; the delicious form was finished with wild oyster mushrooms and sweet cicely flowers.

Not only was the feast locally grounded, but so were the wines I sipped alongside. All came from British Columbia, most from the Okanagan region just east of the Cascade Mountains. They included a white meritage (sauvignon blanc–semillon blend) from Sumac Ridge, the Quails' Gate Family Reserve chardonnay, and a dry white ortega, a less common grape variety, from Venturi-Schulze Vineyards on Vancouver Island. There is a growing synergy among food producers, chefs, and wine makers in British Columbia, and the region's status as a gastronomic destination continues to grow.

Lemongrass Broth with Crab Wontons

There's no aroma quite like either lemongrass or kaffir lime leaves. They are widely available in Asian markets and well-stocked grocers; if you have trouble finding fresh lime leaves, you could add a sliver of lime zest or simply leave the lime element out of this tasty broth. Dried lime leaves aren't as aromatic, in my judgment, so I prefer not to use them in place of fresh.

Those shells you discard after a crab feast can infuse a broth with a richly intense flavor. If you plan ahead, you may rinse and save the shells from just such a meal and freeze them for a week or two before using them. Otherwise, start with whole cooked crab, using its picked meat for the wonton filling (any extra may be frozen for later use) and the shells for the broth. The leg and body shells are all that you need here. In a pinch, you could make the broth without the crab shells, though you'll miss out on the great flavor and aroma they contribute.

Cleaned shells from 2 whole cooked crabs (not including the carapace)	4 stalks lemongrass, trimmed and sliced
2 carrots, sliced	8 to 10 whole black peppercorns
2 stalks celery, sliced	4 cups chicken stock, preferably homemade
2 shallots, sliced	
10 slices ginger	Soy sauce
6 kaffir lime leaves, cut into slivers	¼ cup thinly sliced green onion

Crab Wontons

4 ounces crabmeat	1 teaspoon freshly squeezed lemon juice
3 tablespoons minced green onion	
1 tablespoon minced carrot	1 teaspoon soy sauce
1 tablespoon minced celery	16 thin, square wonton wrappers

Preheat the oven to 375°F. Scatter the crab shells in a baking dish and roast until they are aromatic and lightly browned, about 25 minutes.

Transfer the shells to a small stockpot and add the carrots, celery, shallots, ginger, lime leaves, lemongrass, and peppercorns. If any crab juices are baked onto the baking dish, add a cup of warm water and stir to dissolve them, adding the liquid to the pot. Add the chicken stock with enough cold water to cover the ingredients by an inch or so (about 2 quarts), and bring just to a boil over medium-high heat. Reduce the heat to medium and simmer until aromatic and some of the color of the roasted shells has been imparted to the stock, about 1 hour.

While the broth is simmering, prepare the crab wontons. Pick over the crabmeat to remove any bits of shell or cartilage, and put it in a food processor. Add the green onion, carrot, celery, lemon juice, and soy sauce and pulse a few times to blend and finely chop the mixture, without making a paste. Lay the wonton wrappers out on the work surface and place a tablespoon of the crab filling in the center of each wrapper. Dip your finger in a small bowl of warm water and use it to lightly dampen the edges of the wrappers. Fold each wrapper in half, corner to corner, pressing out as much air as possible and pinching the edges to seal securely. Bring a large pot of well-salted water to a boil.

While the water is heating, line a sieve with a dampened paper towel and set it over a large bowl. Strain the broth through the sieve and discard the shells and vegetables. Return the broth to the pot, season to taste with soy sauce, and keep hot over medium heat.

When the water comes to a rolling boil, add the wontons, reduce the heat to medium, and simmer until they are just tender, 3 to 5 minutes. Drain well and put 4 wontons in each of 4 serving bowls. Ladle the hot broth over the wontons, scatter with the sliced green onion, and serve right away.

Makes 4 servings

Green Goddess Crab and Watercress Sandwiches

The *Green Goddess* was a theatrical presentation before it had a namesake in any dining room. The salad dressing was created at San Francisco's Palace Hotel in 1923 for the play's star, British actor George Arliss, who was staying there during the play's San Francisco run. The herby dressing, with a subtle kick from anchovy, inspires this simple but elegant crab sandwich. For homemade mayonnaise, you may use the Lemon Mayonnaise recipe on page 82, omitting the lemon zest and using only 1 teaspoon of lemon juice.

As an alternative to standard sandwiches, these could be served open-faced on halved or quartered pieces of bread, each topped with a bit of watercress. Or, for more cocktail-like nibbles, you could serve the crab mixture atop toasted baguette slices or crackers. Even better, scoop a bit of the salad into the slender, delicate leaves of Belgian endive, one of the world's perfect edible containers.

½ cup mayonnaise, preferably
   homemade
2 green onions, minced
2 anchovy fillets, finely chopped
2 tablespoons finely chopped flat-leaf
   (Italian) parsley
1 tablespoon minced chives
1 tablespoon tarragon vinegar or
   white wine vinegar

1 teaspoon minced tarragon
Freshly ground black pepper
8 ounces crabmeat
8 thin slices white bread
2 ounces watercress, rinsed, dried,
   and tough stems removed

In a medium bowl, combine the mayonnaise, green onions, anchovy, parsley, chives, vinegar, and tarragon with pepper to taste. Stir to mix evenly, and refrigerate for at least 1 hour to allow the flavors to blend. (The mixture can be made up to 2 days in advance.)

Pick over the crabmeat to remove any bits of shell or cartilage and add it to the dressing. Stir with a fork to mix evenly, and then spoon the crab salad in a thin layer on 4 of the bread slices. Top the salad with the watercress leaves, followed by the remaining bread slices. Cut each sandwich in half diagonally, and serve right away.

Makes 4 servings

Tillamook Cheese: In northwestern Oregon there is a lush and fertile region that Native peoples named Tillamook (today both a city and a county), meaning "land of many waters." The rivers and streams in this area feed pastureland that, in turn, feeds many thousand dairy cows that turn out the exemplary milk of the Tillamook County Creamery Association. Though today this creamery produces a wide variety of cheeses, as well as ice cream, yogurt, and other dairy products, their original cheddar cheese (a century-old recipe) still accounts for more than three-quarters of total dairy production. It is made 365 days a year to keep up with demand. When you're next driving along the northern Oregon coast, you may drop in for a visit . . . and a sample.

Crab and Tillamook Cheddar Sandwiches

Although crab and cheese sandwiches are popular throughout the Northwest, one place that has perfected the concept is the Bait House Cafe in Seattle's Ballard neighborhood. Originally, and still, a place where fishermen buy fresh herring bait, the cafe now has a following of landlubbers who come for the great view of boats on their way to and from the Hiram M. Chittenden Locks, for the live jazz on weekends, and for the signature crab sandwich. Owner Sharon Relei's recipe is a secret, but this recipe is inspired by the Bait House offering, which is often served with a crisp Caesar salad on the side. The cheese may be sharp or medium, depending on your taste.

4 slices sourdough bread

12 ounces crabmeat

2 cups grated Tillamook cheddar
   cheese (about 8 ounces)

¼ cup thinly sliced green onion

4 to 5 tablespoons mayonnaise,
   preferably homemade

Preheat the broiler. Toast the bread slices about 4 inches from the broiler element until lightly browned on one side. Set aside on a wire rack to cool. Keep the broiler on.

Pick over the crabmeat to remove any bits of shell or cartilage, and put it in a medium bowl with the cheese and green onion. Toss to mix, and then add just enough mayonnaise to hold the crab and cheese together; if you add too much, the sandwiches will be soft and soggy. Stir the mixture well to be sure the ingredients are blended and cohesive.

Spread the crab mixture on the untoasted side of the bread slices and place them on a baking sheet. Broil the sandwiches until the cheese is melted and the top is bubbly, 3 to 4 minutes. Transfer the sandwiches to individual plates and serve.

Makes 4 servings

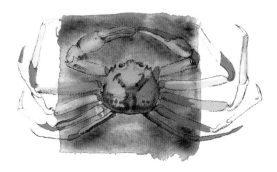

Crab Club Sandwich

Traditionally, club sandwiches have 3 slices of bread each, but I've modified the idea to a conventional 2-slice sandwich in which crab meets up with smoky bacon, sliced tomato, crisp lettuce, and—one of my favorite sandwich embellishments—slices of rich avocado. There's nothing not to like about this sandwich. Just take care to toast the bread only lightly so it doesn't become too crunchy.

Old-fashioned white bread is typical for such a sandwich, but you may use any variety you like. For homemade mayonnaise, you may use the recipe for Lemon Mayonnaise (see page 82), using only 1 teaspoon of lemon juice and omitting the lemon zest.

4 slices bread	6 to 8 ounces crabmeat
2 tablespoons mayonnaise, preferably homemade	½ lemon, cut into 2 wedges
	4 thin slices large beefsteak tomato
2 leaves green lettuce, rinsed and dried	4 slices bacon, fried crisp
	½ ripe but firm avocado

Lightly toast the bread and let it cool. Spread ½ tablespoon of the mayonnaise on one side of each bread slice. Top 2 of the slices of bread with the lettuce leaves. Pick over the crabmeat to remove any bits of shell or cartilage. Scatter the crabmeat evenly over the lettuce leaves and squeeze the lemon wedges over the crab, being careful to remove any seeds that might fall from the lemon. Lay the tomato slices over the crab and top with the bacon. Peel, pit, and thinly slice the avocado half, and lay the slices over the bacon. Top with the remaining bread (mayonnaise side down), cut each sandwich in half diagonally, and serve right away.

Makes 2 servings

Salads

Crab Louis

This time-honored recipe needs no updating, because to do so would make it not a Louis, but just another (albeit delicious) crab salad. The lettuce must be crisp, bright iceberg, the eggs hard-cooked, the tomato cut in wedges. Embellish with artichoke bottoms or blanched asparagus, if you like. And yes, the dressing is at its best made with ketchup or prepared chili sauce. Try to get crabmeat that includes a good portion of whole leg pieces. Or better yet, pick the meat from a couple of crabs yourself to ensure nice big pieces of the sweet meat. Just who the "Louis" is who inspired this classic no one seems to know, though legend leans toward San Francisco as this salad's birthplace. The legacy lives on.

1 head iceberg lettuce, cored, leaves
    separated, rinsed, and dried
8 to 12 ounces crabmeat

4 eggs, hard-cooked, peeled,
    and quartered
2 small tomatoes or 4 plum tomatoes,
    cored and cut into 1-inch wedges

Louis Dressing

¾ cup mayonnaise,
    preferably homemade
⅓ cup chili sauce or ketchup
3 tablespoons finely chopped
    green onion

1 tablespoon minced flat-leaf
    (Italian) parsley
Dash Worcestershire sauce
Dash hot pepper sauce
Salt and freshly ground black pepper

Hard-boiled Eggs: Technically, eggs shouldn't be "hard-boiled." Cooking the eggs at a simmer instead helps to prevent the whites from becoming tough and rubbery. The method I prefer for hard-cooking eggs is to put them in a pan with enough cold water to cover them by about 1 inch. Put the pan over high heat and bring to a boil, then reduce the heat to medium-high and set the timer for 10 minutes. Drain the eggs and run cold water over them for a few minutes to stop the cooking and help cool the eggs quickly. Refrigerate in their shells until ready to serve.

For the Louis dressing, combine the mayonnaise, chili sauce, green onion, parsley, Worcestershire, and hot pepper sauce in a small bowl and stir to mix. Season to taste with salt and pepper and refrigerate until ready to serve.

On 4 chilled plates, arrange a bed of 1 or 2 of the larger lettuce leaves. Cut the remaining lettuce into thin shreds and pile it evenly in the center of each plate. Pick over the crabmeat to remove any bits of shell or cartilage, and arrange it over the shredded lettuce, saving any large leg or body pieces to perch on top. Arrange the egg and tomato wedges evenly around the crab, on the lettuce base. Spoon a bit of the Louis dressing over the crab, passing the rest separately. Serve right away.

Makes 4 servings

Rice Salad with Crab and Asparagus

Fresh spring asparagus, peas, and herbs are ideal complements, both in flavor and color, to rice in this quick and easy salad. The recipe's even quicker if you use leftover steamed white rice—you'll need about 3 cups. The salad could be served on a bed of lettuce, if you like, or in scooped-out whole tomato shells for a retro presentation.

2 cups water
½ teaspoon salt
1 cup long-grain white rice
6 ounces asparagus spears, trimmed
   (halved lengthwise if quite thick)
   and cut into 2-inch pieces
1 cup freshly shelled peas or frozen
   petite peas
8 ounces crabmeat

2 tablespoons minced basil
2 tablespoons minced flat-leaf
   (Italian) parsley
⅓ cup olive oil
¼ cup freshly squeezed lemon juice,
   or more to taste
Salt and freshly ground black pepper
Basil and/or parsley sprigs,
   for garnish

Combine the water and salt in a small saucepan and bring to a boil. Stir in the rice, cover the pan, and cook over low heat until the rice is tender and all the water has been absorbed, 18 to 20 minutes. Take the pan from the heat, fluff the rice with a fork, and set aside to cool completely, stirring occasionally.

Meanwhile, bring a medium saucepan of lightly salted water to a boil and fill a medium bowl with ice water. Add the asparagus pieces to the boiling water and blanch until bright green and just barely tender, 2 to 3 minutes. Scoop out the asparagus with a slotted spoon and put it in the ice water to cool.

Return the water to a boil, add the peas, and cook for 1 to 2 minutes. Drain the peas, add them to the ice water, and let cool completely. Drain the vegetables and scatter them on paper towels to dry.

Put the cooled rice in a large bowl. Pick over the crabmeat to remove any bits of shell or cartilage, and add it to the rice with the asparagus, peas, basil, and parsley. In a small bowl, combine the olive oil and lemon juice with salt and pepper to taste. Whisk to blend, then pour the dressing over the salad, stirring gently to mix evenly. Taste the salad for seasoning, then spoon the salad onto individual plates. Garnish with the herb sprigs and serve.

Makes 4 to 6 servings

Asparagus: The fertile fields and orchards of Eastern Washington produce a wide variety of crops, from lentils, peaches, and sweet onions to the grapes that make the state's award-winning wines. Among the prize harvest each spring is asparagus, grown primarily in the Yakima Valley. Washington is the country's No. 2 producer, just behind California.

When buying asparagus, look for stalks that are plump, not dried or shriveled, with tips that are firm and unblemished. I prefer fatter stalks of asparagus to thin ones, because I find that they have a much more toothsome texture. The base of the spear is generally woody and tough, so should be trimmed off before cooking: simply bend the spear near the bottom of the stalk and it'll snap near the point where the tender part begins.

Crab and Sesame Noodle Salad

In this recipe, tender noodles soak up a flavorful Asian-style vinaigrette, making a tasty base for crabmeat and crisp vegetables. This salad makes a delicious light main course, particularly on a hot summer's day, or serve it alongside a simply grilled piece of fish—salmon would be a particularly good partner.

Somen noodles are thin wheat noodles typically served cold in Japanese cuisine; in the package, they're neatly tied into individual bundles of about 2 ounces each. If you can't find somen noodles, try angel hair pasta instead. Mirin, a sweet Japanese cooking wine made from rice, is available in Asian markets or well-stocked grocery stores alongside soy sauce and other Asian products.

8 ounces somen noodles

2 tablespoons sesame seeds

8 to 12 ounces crabmeat

1 large carrot, cut into julienne strips

1 medium cucumber, halved, peeled, seeded, and thinly sliced

2 tablespoons chopped cilantro

¼ cup sliced green onion tops

Sesame-Soy Dressing

⅓ cup seasoned rice vinegar

¼ cup freshly squeezed lemon juice

¼ cup soy sauce

¼ cup mirin

1 tablespoon finely grated or minced ginger

2 teaspoons Asian sesame oil

Bring a large pot of generously salted water to a boil for cooking the noodles.

While the water is heating, make the dressing. In a small bowl, combine the vinegar, lemon juice, soy sauce, mirin, ginger, and sesame oil and whisk to blend. Set aside.

When the water comes to a rolling boil, add the noodles and cook just until tender, 1 to 2 minutes. Drain the noodles in a colander and run cold water over them to cool them. Drain again well and put the noodles in a large bowl. Whisk the dressing to mix it and drizzle about three-fourths of it over the noodles, tossing to coat them evenly with the dressing. Cover the bowl and refrigerate for at least 1 hour. (The noodles will soak up the dressing as they sit, giving them plenty of flavor.)

Lightly toast the sesame seeds in a small skillet over medium heat until lightly colored and nutty smelling, 3 to 5 minutes. Transfer to a small bowl to cool.

Just before serving, pick over the crabmeat to remove any bits of shell or cartilage, and set aside some larger pieces for garnishing the salad. Add the rest of the crab to the noodles along with the carrot, cucumber, cilantro, and sesame seeds. Toss to mix evenly, and arrange the noodle salad on individual chilled plates. Scatter the sliced green onion over the salad, drizzle with the remaining dressing, and top with the reserved crabmeat. Serve right away.

Makes 4 to 6 servings

Spinach Salad with Crab Toasts and Roasted Onion Vinaigrette

The sharp flavor of raw onion turns slightly sweet when roasted, making a rich base for this tangy vinaigrette dressing. The rich crab toasts served atop the spinach salad finish the dish off with style. It makes a great main course for a lunch or light supper, though it could also be served in smaller portions as a starter salad.

1 cup coarsely chopped onion
4 tablespoons olive oil
4 ounces crabmeat
6 ounces cream cheese,
   at room temperature
Salt and freshly ground black pepper

12 slices baguette bread,
   about ½ inch thick
¼ cup red wine vinegar
1 bunch spinach (about 1 pound),
   rinsed, dried, and tough
   stems removed

Preheat the oven to 375°F. Put the onion in a small baking dish and drizzle 1 tablespoon of the olive oil over it, stirring to coat evenly. Bake the onion until tender and lightly browned, about 30 minutes.

While the onion is roasting, prepare the crab toasts. Pick over the crabmeat to remove any bits of shell or cartilage, and put it in a medium bowl with the cream cheese. Mix with a fork until evenly blended, and then season to taste with salt and pepper.

When the onion is tender, set it aside to cool. Preheat the broiler. Arrange the baguette slices on a baking sheet and toast them about 4 inches from the heat until lightly browned. Take the baking sheet from the oven, turn the slices over, and top the untoasted side of each with the crab mixture, mounding it slightly in the center. Return the sheet to the oven and continue broiling until the crab mixture bubbles and is lightly browned, 2 to 3 minutes. Turn off the broiler and keep the toasts warm on a lower rack in the oven.

Put the cooled onion and the roasting oil in a food processor or blender and purée until smooth. Add the vinegar with the remaining 3 tablespoons olive oil. Purée to blend, and then season to taste with salt and pepper.

Put the spinach leaves in a large bowl, tearing any large leaves in half or thirds. Drizzle the onion vinaigrette over them, and toss to evenly coat. Arrange the spinach on 4 individual plates and top each with 3 crab toasts. Serve right away.

Makes 4 servings

Shaved Fennel Salad with Crab and Blood Oranges

The aromatic citrus flavor of oranges and subtle anisy crunch of fennel makes for a great start to any meal. Blood oranges are a variety of sweet orange that has reddish tones in the flesh that can range from a smattering of red speckles to a solid ruby red. They are available sporadically, and not all markets carry them. Winter into early spring is generally the best time for finding them. Navel oranges, while less colorful, will provide tasty results as well.

2 blood oranges or navel oranges
1 large fennel bulb
4 green onions, thinly sliced
¼ cup olive oil

2 tablespoons red wine vinegar
Salt and freshly ground black pepper
8 ounces crabmeat

Cut both ends from one of the oranges, just to the flesh. Set the orange upright on a cutting board and use the knife to cut away the peel and pith, following the curve of the fruit. Try not to cut away too much of the flesh with the peel.

Working over a medium bowl to catch the juice, hold the peeled orange in your hand and slide the knife blade down one side of a section, cutting it from the membrane. Cut down the other side of the same section and let it fall into the bowl. (Pick out and discard any seeds as you go.) Continue for the remaining sections, turning the flaps of the membrane like the pages of a book. Squeeze the juice from the membrane core into the bowl. Repeat with the second orange.

Trim the root end and stalks of the fennel bulb, reserving some of the feathery fronds. Halve the bulb lengthwise and cut out the tough core. Using a mandoline slicer or a large knife, cut the fennel lengthwise into paper-thin slices, and put them in the bowl with the orange segments. Mince enough of the fennel fronds to measure 1 tablespoon, reserving 4 of the remaining fronds for garnish, and add the minced fennel and green onion to the bowl. Drizzle the olive oil and vinegar over the mixture and season to taste with salt and pepper.

Pick over the crabmeat to remove any bits of shell or cartilage. Add the crab to the salad and toss gently to avoid breaking up the orange pieces. Arrange the salad on chilled plates, drizzling the juices from the bottom of the bowl evenly over the salads. Top with the reserved fennel fronds and serve right away.

Makes 2 to 4 servings

Cucumber and Daikon Sunomono with Crab

The fresh crunch and flavor of cucumber and daikon radish make this an exceptionally refreshing salad, similar to the cucumber sunomono often served at the start of a Japanese meal. Try to find crab that is in nice, plump portions for this salad, to make the most of the contrast between the sweet, meaty crab and the crisp, vinegary vegetables. Picking the meat from a freshly cooked crab may be the best way to be sure that you get large enough pieces, rather than purchasing it in bulk, when the meat is often more flaked.

Shiso, sometimes known as perilla, is an herb related to mint and basil that is commonly used in Japanese cuisine. Its vivid green leaves, with their distinctly toothed edges, are also a common garnish on plates of sushi and sashimi. (There is also a purple shiso, which has leaves that are green on top and purple underneath; its flavor is a little milder than the green shiso.) The subtle anise-mint flavor of shiso adds a distinctive herbal quality to the salad, though you could use parsley or mint in its place.

1 large English cucumber,
    halved and thinly sliced
1 small daikon radish
    (about 8 ounces), peeled
    and thinly sliced
½ small sweet onion, cut into
    thin julienne

1 cup seasoned rice vinegar
1½ teaspoons sugar
1 teaspoon salt
5 to 6 shiso leaves, cut into
    thin julienne
8 ounces crabmeat, preferably
    whole leg and claw pieces

In a large bowl, combine the cucumber, daikon, and onion, and toss to mix evenly.

In a medium bowl, combine the vinegar, sugar, and salt. Let sit for a few minutes, then stir the dressing until the sugar and salt have dissolved. Pour the vinegar mixture over the vegetables, toss well, and set aside for 15 minutes to let them absorb some of the vinegar dressing, stirring a few times. (If the vegetables sit too long, they will begin to lose their crispness; the salad is best made shortly before serving.)

Drain off the dressing into a small dish, then add the shiso to the vegetables and toss to mix evenly. Arrange the vegetables on individual chilled plates, and top with the pieces of crabmeat. Drizzle some of the reserved dressing over all, and serve right away.

Makes 4 to 6 servings

Main Courses

Northwest Crab Boil

Unlike our compatriots in the eastern regions of the country, Northwesterners typically add no spice whatsoever to the pot when boiling crabs for a feast. Why bother? The flavor of the crab itself is near perfection; no seasoning mix is going to make it any better. For shoreside crab boils, locals often cook the crab in seawater, which is clearly quite salty. When boiling crab at home, it's best to use water that's been well salted (about ½ cup per gallon), to replicate the flavor.

A traditional Northwest crab feed dispenses with tablecloths and napkins. Instead, cover the table with newspapers (comics or crossword puzzle in view, if you like, for dinnertime entertainment), and offer plenty of paper towels. It's very much a casual feast, perfect with a chilled local microbrew or crisp regional white wine. Cole slaw, green salad, garlic bread, corn on the cob—pick your favorite fare to serve with the crab.

Depending on your guests' appetites and what else you're serving for dinner, the serving size can range from a half crab to a whole crab per person. If you're increasing this recipe to serve a bigger crowd, keep in mind that you'll need a much bigger pot, or plan to cook the crabs in batches.

2 uncooked Dungeness crabs (about 2 pounds each), live or cleaned and portioned (see page 88)	2 large lemons, cut into wedges, for serving ½ cup unsalted butter, melted, for serving

Bring a large pot (at least 8 quarts) of generously salted water to a boil over high heat. While the water is heating, put the live crabs, if using, into the freezer to dull their senses a bit. (The crabs should be well chilled but should not freeze at all, so don't leave them in the freezer for more than 15 to 20 minutes.) When the water's at a full rolling boil, if you're using live crabs, grab each of them securely at the back of the carapace, and gently but swiftly drop them headfirst into the boiling water. If you're using cleaned crab portions, simply add them to the boiling water. Cover the pot with its lid and return the water to a boil, then reduce the heat to medium-high so the water's actively bubbling but not boiling over. Cook the crabs for 18 to 20 minutes if whole, about 15 minutes for cleaned portions, counting from the time that the water returns to a boil. Keep an eye on the pot during cooking; the liquid may bubble up and over the edge, so you might want to set the lid just askew to allow a bit of steam to escape.

Drain the crabs well. If you cooked portioned crabs, arrange the pieces on a large serving platter with lemon wedges around the edges. If you cooked whole crabs, clean and portion them before serving. Pour the melted butter into individual dishes for each diner, and pass the crab while still warm.

Makes 2 to 4 servings

The Best Crab Cakes with Three Sauces

The recipe for success when it comes to crab cakes is pretty simple: it's all about the crab. Any other ingredients (such as bread crumbs) should simply help hold the cakes together or offer the slightest hint of color or flavor contrast. For my taste, ingredients such as bell pepper are far too overpowering in flavor to include in crab cakes. Instead, you'll find here the more mellow flavorings of celery, green onion, and parsley, which enhance but don't overwhelm the sweet crab. For elegant cocktail party fare, you could form the cakes into smaller rounds, about 1 inch across, and serve them on platters with toothpicks, the sauces alongside for dipping.

I offer three sauce options, depending on your taste and the style of menu the crab cakes will be served with. Rouille (which means "rust" in French) is a rich, garlicky sauce often served with bouillabaisse; the Tarragon Tartar Sauce is a fresh herbal variation on the classic; and the Rhubarb Compote is a springtime option that's rosy pink and decidedly tart.

Rouille, Tarragon Tartar Sauce, or
   Rhubarb Compote (recipes follow)
1 pound crabmeat
About 3 cups fresh bread crumbs
2 egg whites or 1 whole egg, beaten
¼ cup minced celery

2 green onions, minced
2 tablespoons minced flat-leaf
   (Italian) parsley
Freshly ground black pepper
Vegetable oil, for frying

Make the sauce of your choice and refrigerate until ready to serve. (Any of them can be made a day in advance.)

Pick over the crabmeat, removing any bits of shell or cartilage. In a large bowl, combine the crab, 1 cup of the bread crumbs, egg whites (or whole egg), celery, green onions, and parsley, with pepper to taste, and stir to mix evenly. Form the mixture into twelve 3-inch cakes, pressing the cakes firmly so that the mixture holds together. Lightly coat each side with bread crumbs and set aside on a tray coated in more bread crumbs. The cakes will hold together better when fried if they sit in the refrigerator, covered with plastic wrap, for an hour or so before cooking.

Heat about ¼ inch of oil in a large, heavy skillet, preferably nonstick, over medium heat. Fry the crab cakes in batches until nicely browned and heated through, 3 to 5 minutes on each side. Drain briefly on paper towels and keep warm in a low oven while frying the rest, adding more oil to the pan as needed. Serve the crab cakes warm, passing the desired sauce separately.

Makes 4 servings

Rouille

1 small red bell pepper
1 slice white bread, crusts removed
½ cup milk
3 cloves garlic, crushed
1 egg yolk

2 teaspoons white wine vinegar
Pinch dried red pepper flakes
Salt
¾ cup olive oil (not extra virgin)

Roast the red pepper over a gas flame or under the broiler until the skin blackens, turning occasionally to roast evenly, about 10 minutes total. Put the pepper in a plastic bag, seal securely, and set aside to cool. While the pepper is cooling, tear the bread into pieces, put it in a small bowl, and pour the milk over it; set aside to soak.

When the pepper is cool enough to handle, peel away and discard the skin. Remove the core and seeds, and coarsely chop the pepper. Put the pepper in a food processor with the garlic and pulse to chop finely. Squeeze the excess milk from the soaked bread and add the bread to the food processor with the egg yolk, vinegar, pepper flakes, and a generous pinch of salt. Process to blend evenly, scraping down the sides a couple of times. With the motor running, add the olive oil in a slow, steady stream. Transfer the rouille to a bowl and taste for seasoning, adding more salt if necessary. Refrigerate until ready to serve; the sauce will thicken slightly when chilled.

Makes about 1½ cups

Tarragon Tartar Sauce

For the homemade mayonnaise, you could use the recipe for Lemon Mayonnaise on page 82, omitting the lemon zest and using only 1 teaspoon of the lemon juice.

1 cup mayonnaise,
   preferably homemade
¼ cup finely chopped cornichon
   or dill pickle

1 tablespoon tarragon vinegar or
   white wine vinegar
1 tablespoon coarsely chopped capers
1 tablespoon minced tarragon
Salt and freshly ground black pepper

In a small bowl, combine the mayonnaise, pickle, vinegar, capers, and tarragon and stir well to blend. Season to taste with salt and pepper and refrigerate until ready to serve, preferably at least an hour in advance to allow the flavors to blend and develop. Taste the sauce again just before serving, adjusting the seasoning if needed.

Makes about 1¼ cups

Rhubarb Compote

2 tablespoons olive oil
½ cup chopped onion
2 cups peeled, chopped rhubarb
   (about 3 stalks)

1 tablespoon sugar, more if needed
½ cup dry red wine
Salt and freshly ground black pepper

Heat the olive oil in a small skillet over medium heat. Add the onion and sauté until it begins to soften, 2 to 3 minutes. Stir in the rhubarb and continue to sauté, stirring often, until the rhubarb is nearly tender, 5 to 7 minutes. Stir in the sugar until well blended, and then add the wine. Increase the heat to medium-high and cook, stirring occasionally, until the liquid is reduced and thickened, 8 to 10 minutes. Season the compote to taste with salt and pepper. If it is too tart, add a bit more sugar. The compote can be served at room temperature or chilled.

Makes about 1½ cups

The West Coast Crab Feed

Think "pinnacle Dungeness dining experience" and most people on the West Coast will tell you about crab feed traditions with family and friends: the Thanksgiving or Christmas Eve dinner table that is always piled high with freshly steamed crabs or the summer ritual of gathering at the beach house to eat your fill of just-caught Dungeness. Longtime Bay Area resident Bruce Aidells recalls numerous crab feeds enjoyed with his good friend, the late Loni Kuhn, a well-loved San Francisco cooking teacher. At her home, Bruce recalls, there were two simple crab feed rules. "No. 1, no dipping of bread into the melted butter." Reasonable enough. "No. 2, no grabbing of picked crab from your neighbor's plate." Well, okay, but that's no fun!

Up in Washington State, Hoquiam native Pansy Bray can put out a crab feed dinner with the ease that other cooks make meatloaf. Pansy grew up surrounded by seafood, not only because of geography (Hoquiam sits on Grays Harbor, one of the state's most important estuaries for juvenile crab development) but also thanks to her fisherman-processor father, Roy Stritmatter. Early on she graduated from helping pull seaweed from nets to "shaking" crab from shells for her father's business. "It's all in the wrist," says Pansy, who has demonstrated her crab-shaking technique countless times over the years. Today, she contents herself with shaking crab onto her own dinner plate during crab feeds at home. Her two cats enjoy a feast of their own: the upside-down carapaces from which to lap up the crab butter.

But crab feeds in the West have a very public presence as well. Dozens upon dozens of crab feeds are held up and down the coast each year, from Chamber of Commerce community events to church or Elks Club fund-raisers to school reunion festivities. Not only is crab simply a delicious thing to feast on, but there's something socially engaging about dining crab-feed style. For one, all pretense of formality is left at the door. It's a roll-up-your-sleeves-and-eat-with-your-hands extravaganza that puts everyone on an even playing field. You're at the table for a good while, rhythmically cracking the shells, picking out the meat, and relishing each bite, with intermittent swigs of beer or forkfuls of cole slaw. This is gastronomic social interaction at its very best.

Most crab feeds tend to be held in winter and early spring, when the newly opened season means good stocks of crab and the lowest prices of the year. George Santilena of Buz's Crab, a seafood market and restaurant in Redding, California, has made a significant side business of selling crab-feed packages to organizations in the West. They can range in size from a minimum of 100 pounds to as much as 15,000 pounds of crab for a single event; "there are a couple each year that are that big," Santilena says. Though Redding is about 150 miles inland from the ocean coast, Buz's stays well stocked in fresh crab thanks to near daily trips to collect the crustaceans live from crabbers in the Eureka and Crescent City area. In addition to the main attraction of cooked whole crab (which are freshly cooked for each crab feed order), Buz's provides bibs, clam chowder, sourdough bread (they make their own), and a trio of sauces: cocktail, Louis, and tartar.

Picker or Piler? The world of crab-eaters can be split into two distinct groups: pickers and pilers. The pickers enjoy the fruits of their labor as they go, while pilers are those who get all the hard work done first and hedonistically relish the big heap of ready-to-eat meat when the work's complete. I, for one, am a picker, too eager to enjoy the luscious meat to wait. Surely this phenomenon could make an interesting thesis subject for some future psychologist.

Crab and Italian Sausage Cioppino

Bruce Aidells is just the guy to take a San Francisco classic such as cioppino and make it his own without rocking the boat. He's lived in the Bay Area for more than forty years, so he knows a little something about Dungeness crab and the Italian heritage of the region that led to this marriage of crab with tomato sauce, a quintessential seafood stew. But he's also a chef and sausage maker by trade. His embellishment? Hot Italian sausage. You'll be surprised at how well the spicy, rich meat blends with the tomatoes, herbs, and crab. You could use mild sausage instead if you prefer.

Although it's virtually always based on Dungeness crab, cioppino often includes other types of seafood as well. Bruce's original recipe added a few dozen clams or mussels and a couple of pounds of halibut cut into cubes. You may do the same, reducing the number of crabs from three to one, but I have always preferred crab-only renderings of cioppino myself. Sourdough bread is *de rigueur* with this redolent crab stew, as are plenty of napkins.

1 tablespoon olive oil
1½ pounds hot or mild Italian sausages
1 cup chopped onion
⅓ cup diced celery
1 cup thinly sliced green onion
½ cup diced green bell pepper
3 tablespoons minced garlic
1 pound fresh Italian plum tomatoes,
    peeled, seeded, and coarsely
    chopped, or 2 cups coarsely
    chopped canned Italian-style
    tomatoes
2 cups fish stock or chicken stock,
    preferably homemade
1 cup bottled clam juice
½ cup dry red wine

¼ cup tomato paste
¼ cup freshly squeezed lemon juice,
    or more to taste
4 bay leaves
2 teaspoons minced basil,
    or ½ teaspoon dried
2 teaspoons minced thyme,
    or ½ teaspoon dried
3 Dungeness crabs (about 2 pounds
    each), cleaned and portioned
    (see page 88), shells lightly cracked
    if precooked
Salt and freshly ground black pepper
Lemon slices, for garnish
¼ cup chopped flat-leaf (Italian)
    parsley, for garnish

Heat the olive oil in a large pot or Dutch oven (about 8 quarts) over medium heat. Add the sausages whole and fry until they are firm and lightly browned, turning them often, about 10 minutes. Set the sausages aside to cool; if there are more than 2 or 3 tablespoons of fat in the pot, spoon out and discard the excess.

Add the onion and celery and cook until tender and aromatic, about 5 minutes, stirring occasionally. Add the green onion, bell pepper, and garlic and cook for 2 minutes longer.

Cut the sausages into 1-inch pieces and put them back in the pot along with the tomatoes, stock, clam juice, wine, tomato paste, lemon juice, bay leaves, basil, and thyme. Bring just to a boil over high heat, reduce the heat to medium-low, and simmer for 10 minutes. Add the crab pieces, cover the pot, and cook until the shells are bright red and the flesh is cooked through, 15 to 20 minutes for raw crab (pick into a couple of the thicker sections of body meat to check for doneness), or 10 to 12 minutes for precooked crab.

Season the cioppino to taste with salt, pepper, and more lemon juice. Remove the bay leaves and discard. Serve at once in large, shallow bowls, garnishing each bowl with a slice of lemon and a sprinkling of parsley.

Makes 6 to 8 servings

Crab and Chanterelle Risotto

The sweet chewiness of crabmeat offers a distinct contrast to the nutty rice and earthy mushrooms in this risotto recipe. The Northwest's crop of wild chanterelles is at its peak in the damp, mild fall and generally continues until the first frost. When chanterelles aren't available, you may use shiitake, crimini, or even white button mushrooms instead.

4 tablespoons unsalted butter
8 to 12 ounces chanterelle mushrooms,
    wiped clean, trimmed,
    and thinly sliced
1 cup dry white wine
3 cups chicken stock,
    preferably homemade

½ cup finely chopped onion
1 cup Carnaroli or Arborio rice
12 ounces crabmeat
Salt and freshly ground black pepper
2 tablespoons minced flat-leaf
    (Italian) parsley

Melt 2 tablespoons of the butter in a medium skillet over medium-high heat. Add the mushrooms and sauté, stirring frequently, until they are tender and lightly browned, 5 to 7 minutes. Transfer the mushrooms to a bowl and set aside.

Add the white wine to the skillet and stir just to draw up any remaining cooking juices and flavors from the mushrooms, then pour the wine into a medium saucepan. Add the chicken stock to the saucepan with the wine and bring just to a boil over medium-high heat. Immediately reduce the heat to low and keep warm.

Melt the remaining 2 tablespoons butter in a medium, heavy saucepan over medium heat, add the onion, and stir until tender and aromatic, about 3 minutes. The onion should soften but not brown. Add the rice and stir gently until it is evenly blended with the onion. Scoop about 1 cup of the warm chicken stock into the rice and cook, stirring constantly, until the rice has absorbed most of the liquid, 3 to 5 minutes. Repeat the process once more, adding another cup of liquid. Continue adding the stock, ½ cup at a time, stirring the rice constantly until most of the liquid is absorbed before adding the next, until the risotto is thick and creamy and the rice tender but not too soft—there should still be a bit of resistance at the center of each grain. You may not need every drop of the stock; total cooking time will be 30 to 40 minutes.

Pick over the crabmeat to remove any bits of shell or cartilage; if using king or snow crab meat, cut the shelled leg portions into ¼-inch pieces. Add the crab to the risotto along with the sautéed mushrooms and stir just to warm them through. Season the risotto to taste with salt and pepper, spoon it into warmed shallow bowls, and sprinkle the parsley over it. Serve right away.

Makes 4 servings

Steamed King Crab with Garlic

This recipe is my interpretation of half of the elaborate king crab feast I had with friends at Sun Sui Wah Seafood Restaurant in Vancouver, British Columbia (see page 81). There, only the leg portions were used, but both leg and body portions will work just fine. Unless you're lucky enough to find freshly cooked king crab legs at your store, buy frozen king crab portions and keep them frozen until the day before you're ready to use them. Thaw the crab overnight in the refrigerator. Be prepared for them to give off a lot of liquid as they thaw. I suggest putting them in a baking dish (such as a 9-by-13-inch dish) for thawing. You could also use portioned, precooked Dungeness crab, lightly cracking the shells first to allow the garlicky flavors to penetrate the meat.

A two-layer bamboo steamer rack (an inexpensive kitchen addition, available at cookware stores and Asian markets) is the best vessel for steaming the crab legs, which should be able to lie flat so that the garlic paste will stay in place. The steamer basket is designed to sit snugly in a wok for steaming, though you may also perch it over a pot of the same diameter as the basket.

¼ cup chopped garlic (8 to 10 cloves)
2 tablespoons chopped green onion
1 tablespoon Asian sesame oil
2 teaspoons Shaoxing wine
    (Chinese rice wine), dry sherry,
    or dry white wine

¼ teaspoon salt
2 pounds thawed king crab portions

Combine the garlic and green onion in a mini-processor or blender and pulse to mix. Add the sesame oil, wine, and salt and process until the mixture forms a thick purée, scraping down the sides of the bowl as needed. It will take 30 to 60 seconds for this purée to form. Alternatively, you could make the paste with a mortar and pestle.

Put a few inches of water in the bottom of a wok or large pot over which a bamboo steamer basket will fit snugly. Bring the water to a boil over high heat.

While the water is heating, use a cleaver or other large, heavy knife to cut the longer crab legs into pieces about 6 inches long (or simply in half). Using the same knife or heavy kitchen shears, split the length of the shell (just on one side, not all the way through) to allow flavors to penetrate the meat and make extracting the crabmeat easier.

Spoon the garlic paste over the crab pieces, spreading it lightly across the split opening with the back of the spoon. Lay the crab pieces on 2 heatproof plates that will fit inside the steamer baskets, and stack the baskets over the boiling water. Cover and steam until the crab is heated through and the aroma of garlic permeates the basket, about 10 minutes. Transfer the crab leg portions to individual plates, and serve right away.

Makes 2 to 4 servings

Garlic: As garlic ages, a germ develops in the center of each clove—the little sprouts you sometimes see poking from the bottom of a head of garlic. The garlic is still fine to use when this happens, though the flavor is a bit coarser than that of fresh garlic. It is best to discard that germ before preparing the clove as needed: simply cut the clove in half lengthwise and use the tip of the knife to lift out the germ.

Beer-Steamed Crab with Mustard Butter

The Northwest has a long tradition of beer making, so it seems natural to combine the earthy, yeasty flavor of local microbrew with the sweet, briny flavor of local crab. With a touch of fresh herbs and hints of spice from dried chiles, this simple steamed crab recipe has a bit more flavor than the classic crab boil. You may use live or precooked crab, although raw crab will absorb more flavor from the steam than cooked crab will.

½ cup unsalted butter
½ teaspoon mustard powder
2 bottles (12 ounces each) pale ale
3 to 4 dried red chiles, or ½ teaspoon
    dried red pepper flakes
2 bay leaves, preferably fresh,
    torn or crushed

4 to 5 sprigs flat-leaf (Italian) parsley
2 Dungeness crabs (about 2 pounds
    each), cleaned and portioned
    (see page 88), shells lightly cracked
    if precooked

Melt the butter in a small saucepan over medium heat. Take the pan off the heat, stir in the mustard powder, and set aside.

Pour the ale into a large pot (about 8-quart capacity), add the chiles, bay leaves, and parsley sprigs, and set a collapsible steamer basket in the bottom of the pot. Cover the pot and bring the beer to a boil over high heat. Add the crab portions, cover, reduce the heat to medium-high, and steam until the crab is cooked through, 12 to 15 minutes. (If using precooked crab, steam until it is just heated through, about 7 to 10 minutes.) Check the level of liquid once or twice toward the end of cooking to be certain that the pan's not steaming dry; if the liquid is nearly evaporated, add a cup or so of very hot (preferably boiling) water to the pot.

Transfer the steamed crab portions to individual plates. Stir the mustard butter to gently remix, and pour it into individual dishes. Have a bowl available for discarded shells, and provide plenty of napkins.

Makes 2 to 4 servings

Wokked Pea Vines with Crab and Ginger

Pea vines have long been prized in Asian cuisines and are becoming a favorite of Northwest cooks and diners as well. In this dish, the fresh, bright pea vines, which have a subtle, sweet pea flavor, pair beautifully with crab and the vibrant flavor of fresh ginger, which is both in the sauce and fried for garnishing the dish. If you cannot find fresh pea vines, available primarily in well-stocked produce departments or at Asian markets, you may use about a pound of snow peas, trimmed and lightly steamed or boiled, instead.

Peanut oil or vegetable oil, for frying
2 tablespoons julienned ginger
½ cup fish stock or chicken stock, preferably homemade
1 tablespoon cornstarch
8 ounces crabmeat

12 ounces pea vines, rinsed, tough stems trimmed
2 tablespoons minced ginger
¾ cup sliced green onion
½ cup sake or dry vermouth
2 tablespoons soy sauce

Heat about 1 inch of oil in a small saucepan over medium-high heat. When hot (test with a piece of julienned ginger; the oil should bubble vigorously around it when added), add the julienned ginger and fry until just lightly browned and crisp, about 1 minute. Using a slotted spoon, transfer the fried ginger to paper towels to drain; set aside, reserving the oil. In a small dish, combine the stock and cornstarch and stir to mix; set aside. Pick over the crabmeat to remove any bits of shell or cartilage.

Scoop 2 tablespoons of the frying oil carefully from the saucepan into a wok or large, heavy skillet. Heat the oil over medium-high heat, add about half of the pea vines, and stir-fry until tender and bright green, 2 to 3 minutes. Transfer the pea vines to a serving platter and set aside. Stir-fry the remaining pea vines, adding a bit more oil to the wok if needed, then add them to the platter. Keep the pea vines warm in a low oven while preparing the sauce.

Add another tablespoon of oil to the wok, add the minced ginger, and cook until aromatic, about 30 seconds. Add the green onion, cook for about 1 minute longer, and then add the sake and the stock-cornstarch mixture (stirred first to remix). Reduce the heat to medium and cook until the sauce is thickened, 3 to 5 minutes, stirring often. Add the crab and soy sauce and taste for seasoning, adding more soy sauce to taste. Spoon the crab sauce over the pea vines on the serving platter, scatter the fried ginger on top, and serve right away.

Makes 4 servings

Salt and Pepper Crab

This is one of my all-time favorite crab dishes, based on a signature recipe from Seattle's Flying Fish restaurant. It will have you delightedly slurping crabmeat from its shells and licking your fingers. For big appetites, double the quantity of crab and spices, serving a whole crab per person. At Flying Fish, the chefs first boil the live crab for just 4 minutes to kill it, and then clean the crab and reserve the crab "butter" for stirring into the stir-fry toward the end. You may certainly do the same if you like, though I've simplified the recipe slightly to start with cleaned and portioned crab.

Szechwan pepper—both highly aromatic and spicy—is not related to black pepper but is instead the dried berry of the prickly ash tree. You'll find it in specialty spice or Asian markets. Fish sauce is a pungent, salty liquid with an amber tone that is used in Southeast Asia much the way soy sauce is used in China and Japan. In Vietnam it goes by the name *nuac nam,* while Thai cooks know it as *nam pla;* by either name, the sauce is available in well-stocked grocery stores.

1 teaspoon kosher salt	¼ cup peanut oil or vegetable oil
1 teaspoon freshly ground black pepper	1 Dungeness crab (about 2 pounds), cleaned and portioned
1 teaspoon lightly crushed Szechwan pepper	(see page 88), shells lightly cracked if precooked

Nam Pla Prik

¼ cup fish sauce	6 Thai green chiles, chopped
¼ cup freshly squeezed lime juice	1 clove garlic, minced

For the Nam Pla Prik sauce, combine the fish sauce, lime juice, chiles, and garlic in a small bowl, stir to mix, and set aside. The sauce can be made a day or two in advance and refrigerated until ready to serve. Keep in mind, however, that the longer the sauce sits, the more heat it will take on from the chiles.

In a small dish, combine the salt, black pepper, and Szechwan pepper and stir to mix. Heat the oil in a wok or large, heavy skillet over medium-high heat until it is almost smoking. Carefully add the crab pieces and, if using uncooked crab, stir-fry until the shells are bright red and the meat turns from translucent to opaque (use the body meat to judge for doneness; its flesh will be more visible), about 5 minutes. If using cooked crab, stir-fry until it is heated through, 2 to 3 minutes. Sprinkle the spice mixture over the crab and continue stir-frying until it is evenly coated in the spices and they give off a slightly toasty aroma, about 1 minute longer.

Transfer the crab to a warmed serving platter and pour the Nam Pla Prik into individual bowls for dipping. Have a discard bowl available for shells, and provide plenty of napkins.

Makes 2 servings

Fresh Noodles with Crab and Cilantro

Despite the fact that fresh pasta is available in many markets today, there really is nothing better than pasta you've made yourself and cooked shortly after rolling and cutting the dough. Here the dough contains cilantro, adding a vibrant green color as well as a fresh herbal flavor to the noodles. Whole leaves of the same herb are tossed with the steaming noodles, crab, and sweet butter for a simple but sophisticated finish. For a super shortcut, or if you don't have a pasta machine, you could use top-quality imported dry fettuccine in place of the fresh pasta.

1¼ cups all-purpose flour, plus more
    as needed for rolling out pasta
½ teaspoon salt
2 eggs
2 tablespoons chopped cilantro
8 to 12 ounces crabmeat

6 tablespoons unsalted butter,
    cut into pieces
1 cup moderately packed
    cilantro leaves
Freshly ground white pepper

Put the flour in a food processor with the salt and pulse once to blend. Add the eggs and pulse to blend, then add the chopped cilantro and pulse one last time. Transfer the dough to the counter, form it into a ball, and knead it for a few minutes to create a cohesive, satiny dough. Wrap the dough in plastic and set it aside on the counter for about 30 minutes.

Cut the pasta dough in half. Flatten one of the halves with the heel of your hand, lightly dust it with flour, and roll it through the widest setting of a pasta machine. Fold the ends inward so that the packet is about 4 inches across, and run the pasta through the rollers again, with the folded edges at either side. Repeat this process 6 to 8 more times to further knead the dough and make it very smooth, dusting the dough lightly with flour as needed. Decrease the roller width by one setting and pass the full length of the pasta sheet through the rollers. Continue rolling out the dough at thinner and thinner settings until it is about 1/16 inch thick.

Drape the pasta on a pasta rack or over the back of a chair that has been covered with a dishcloth. Repeat the rolling process with the remaining dough. Let the dough sheets rest for about 10 minutes before continuing.

Scatter about 1/4 cup flour on a rimmed baking sheet. Cut the first sheet of dough in half crosswise to make it easier to handle, and then pass each half through the wider fettuccine blades of the pasta cutter. Set the noodles in a nest on the floured baking sheet, tossing gently to be sure they don't stick together. Repeat with the remaining dough. Bring a large pot of generously salted water to a boil.

While the water's heating, pick over the crabmeat to remove any bits of shell or cartilage.

When the water is at a full boil, add the noodles and boil just until al dente, about 1 minute. Drain the pasta well. Set the empty pasta pot back over medium heat, and let it sit for a few moments, until all the water has evaporated from the pot. Add the butter and stir until mostly melted, then add the drained pasta and toss gently to coat it evenly with the butter. Add the cilantro leaves and crab, with salt and pepper to taste, and toss to mix. Transfer the pasta to a large warmed bowl, and serve right away.

Makes 4 to 6 servings

Crab à la James Beard: One of the more famous sons of the Northwest, at least among the food-loving crowd, is the inimitable James Beard. He was a figure larger than life in many senses. Growing up in Portland, Oregon, and spending much of his childhood on the state's ocean beaches, Beard acquired an early love for foods of the Northwest, an appreciation that lasted through his life and found its way into many of his writings about food.

My cookbook shelves groan with hundreds of books collected over the years, but one I am more likely to pick up than most is Beard's *American Cookery,* published in 1972. In it he offers a variety of crab recipes, which tend toward the Northwest premise of "simpler is better." His Classic Crab Salad starts with a base of watercress or Boston lettuce, which he tops with a generous pile of "the choicest crabmeat available" and serves with homemade mayonnaise, hard-cooked eggs, ripe olives, and cherry tomatoes. A timeless classic, indeed.

King Crab in Two Courses

Not too many years ago, virtually all king crab commercially harvested in Alaska was cooked right after being caught, then frozen for distribution in that icy state. But today, some of those huge, leggy crabs are making their way to markets and restaurants alive, giving us consumers a chance to enjoy succulent, freshly cooked king crab without having to make the long trip to the crab's homeland in the Last Frontier.

I enjoyed the fruits of this new live-crab commute one cold, gray day in Vancouver, British Columbia at Sun Sui Wah Seafood Restaurant, where huge saltwater tanks hold a variety of live seafoods for the picking. There were eight of us around the large table and we were first shown our crab live on a large platter, while manager Allan Yung explained that the eight-pound crab would be presented in two courses. Hearing of the garlic paste and sesame oil, the steaming and the frying, the chile peppers and coarse salt didn't seem to unnerve that great beast, though it did put our taste buds in gear.

First, the fat legs were split and steamed with a simple, heady garlic paste. The steaming legs were piled on a huge platter and topped with the beautiful carapace, giving an impression of the crab in peaceful (albeit garlicky) repose. I don't think the lazy Susan could have spun fast enough to get that platter around to everyone in time. (My own interpretation of this part of the meal can be found on page 74.)

Next, the body meat was served still in its white papery shell, the pieces quickly fried in a floury coating with only chile peppers and salt for embellishment. Talk about finger-licking good! We picked apart that coating, both literally and figuratively, trying to decide if it was all-purpose flour or rice flour, or maybe it was cornstarch? Wrong, wrong, and wrong. During our post-feast tour through the bustling kitchen (a wedding party was due to start shortly thereafter), we learned the truth: those king crab pieces had met with none other than Bird's Custard Powder, an English kitchen staple which is basically cornstarch with salt and flavorings.

Even now, I have vivid taste memories of that outstanding meal. If you find yourself with an opportunity to taste king crab freshly cooked, I highly recommend that you splurge at least once on this great delicacy.

King Crab

Cold Cracked Crab with Lemon Mayonnaise

This is about as simple as it gets: freshly cooked Dungeness crab, served chilled and ready to eat. Tuck a napkin under your chin, and have a glass of crisp white wine within easy reach. Serving the crab cold rather than hot and fresh from the pot not only saves you from the risk of burning your fingers but also means that the meat slips more easily from the shells.

Making mayonnaise by hand, with just a bowl and a whisk, is quite rewarding, although it does take some dexterity to hold the bowl and drizzle the oil with one hand while whisking madly with the other. One trick involves a kitchen towel: Grab the towel by opposite corners and twist them to make a long, slender roll, then wrap the roll around the base of the mixing bowl, gently tying the ends to secure it. This will help keep the bowl from bouncing around too much as you work. I've offered a quick and foolproof food processor option as well.

2 uncooked Dungeness crabs
   (about 2 pounds each),
   live or cleaned and portioned
   (see page 88)

Lemon wedges, for serving

Lemon Mayonnaise

1 small lemon
1 egg yolk

¾ cup olive oil (not extra virgin)
Salt and freshly ground white pepper

For the lemon mayonnaise, finely grate enough zest from the lemon to measure ½ teaspoon and set it aside, then squeeze the juice from the lemon (you should have about 2 tablespoons). In a medium bowl, combine 1 teaspoon of the lemon juice with the egg yolk and whisk to blend. Begin adding the olive oil, a drop at a time, whisking constantly, until the yolk begins to turn pale and thicken slightly, showing that an emulsion has begun to form. Continue adding the rest of the oil in a thin, steady stream, whisking constantly. Whisk in the remaining lemon juice with the lemon zest and salt and white pepper to taste. Alternatively, combine the teaspoon of lemon juice and egg yolk in a food processor and pulse to blend. With the motor running, begin adding the oil a few drops at a time, then continue adding the rest in a thin, steady stream. Add the remaining lemon juice with the lemon zest and salt and pepper to taste and pulse to blend. Refrigerate the mayonnaise, covered, until ready to serve;

it will have a fuller, more balanced flavor if made at least an hour before serving, and it can be made a day or two in advance.

Bring a large pot (at least 8 quarts) of generously salted water to a boil over high heat. While the water is heating, put the live crabs, if using, into the freezer to dull their senses a bit. (The crabs should be well chilled but should not freeze at all, so don't leave them in the freezer for more than 15 or 20 minutes.) When the water's at a full rolling boil, if you're using live crabs, grab each of them securely at the back of the carapace, and gently but swiftly drop them headfirst into the boiling water. If you're using cleaned crab portions, simply add them to the boiling water. Cover the pot with its lid and return the water to a boil, then reduce the heat to medium-high so the water's actively bubbling but not boiling over. Cook the crabs for 18 to 20 minutes if whole, about 15 minutes for cleaned portions, counting from the time the water returns to a boil. Keep an eye on the pot during cooking; the liquid may bubble up and over the edge, so you might want to set the lid just askew to allow a bit of steam to escape.

Carefully drain the crabs and cool them under cold running water or in a sinkful of ice water, then pat them dry and refrigerate until well chilled, 1 to 2 hours. When cold, clean and portion the whole crabs (see page 88), and arrange the pieces on a large platter or on individual plates, with the lemon wedges alongside. Pass the lemon mayonnaise separately, or serve it in individual bowls for each diner.

Makes 2 to 4 servings

Stir-Fried Crab with Asian Black Bean Sauce

This versatile recipe can be adapted to use cooked Dungeness crab portions or sections of snow or king crab legs, though precooked crab will need to be just heated through, so reduce the crab stir-frying time to just a few minutes. Be sure to lightly crack or split the leg portions before cooking, to allow the sauce flavors to get at the meat. Cut really long legs into manageable (about 6-inch) pieces to make stir-frying easier.

Fermented black beans (also known as salted black beans) are pungent in flavor and quite salty, so a little goes a long way. Look for them in Asian markets or on well-stocked grocery shelves. Along with the aromatics of ginger, garlic, and green onion, they create an addictive complement to the sweet crabmeat. It is something of a messy proposition, so have plenty of napkins on hand. Simple steamed white rice and steamed snowpeas would be ideal accompaniments to this flavorful crab dish.

¼ cup sake or dry sherry

2 tablespoons coarsely chopped fermented black beans

2 teaspoons cornstarch

3 tablespoons vegetable oil

2 whole dried red chiles

1 uncooked Dungeness crab (about 2 pounds), cleaned and portioned (see page 88), or 1½ pounds king or snow leg portions, thawed

½ cup sliced green onion

2 tablespoons minced ginger

2 teaspoons minced garlic

¼ cup fish stock or water

2 tablespoons soy sauce

1 teaspoon sugar

¼ teaspoon dried red pepper flakes, more to taste

In a small bowl, combine the sake and black beans and let sit for at least 30 minutes. Add the cornstarch to the sake and black beans and stir to mix.

Heat the oil in a wok or large skillet over medium-high heat. Add the chiles and cook, stirring, until fragrant and well-browned, about 30 seconds. Remove the chiles and discard them. Carefully add the crab pieces and, if using uncooked crab, stir-fry until the shells are bright red and the meat turns from translucent to opaque (use the body meat to judge doneness; its flesh will be more visible), about 5 minutes. If using cooked crab, stir-fry until it is heated through, 2 to 3 minutes. Add the green onion, ginger, and garlic to the wok and stir-fry until they are nearly tender and the mixture is aromatic, 2 to 3 minutes longer.

Stir the sake and black bean mixture and add it to the wok with the fish stock, soy sauce, and sugar. Stir until the sauce is thickened and evenly coats the crab, 1 to 2 minutes.

Sprinkle with the pepper flakes and taste for seasoning, adding more pepper flakes or soy sauce if needed.

Scoop the crab and sauce onto individual plates and serve immediately, with a discard bowl available for shells and plenty of napkins.

Makes 2 servings

Rosemary Roasted Crab

The rosemary, lemon, and garlic roasted with the crab in this dish penetrate the sweet meat with delicious subtlety while filling the kitchen with their aroma. This preparation is particularly good with raw crab portions, which will absorb the flavors more than precooked crabmeat will. If using king crab leg portions, partially split the shells before roasting, to allow the flavors to penetrate and to make shelling them easier for your guests.

2 Dungeness crabs (about 2 pounds
   each), cleaned and portioned
   (see page 88), shells lightly cracked
   if precooked, or 1½ pounds thawed
   king or snow leg portions
6 to 8 long sprigs rosemary
   (about 1½ ounces)

1 large lemon, thinly sliced
¼ cup olive oil
4 cloves garlic, chopped
¼ teaspoon dried red pepper flakes
Salt and freshly ground black pepper

Preheat the oven to 450°F.

Lay the crab portions in a 9-by-13-inch baking dish and top with the rosemary sprigs and lemon slices. Add the olive oil, garlic, and pepper flakes, and season generously with salt and pepper. Toss to coat the crab pieces evenly with the seasonings, arranging them finally in an even layer with most of the rosemary and lemon underneath. Roast the crab until the flesh is just opaque through (use body portions to judge; their flesh will be more visible), about 15 minutes for raw crab, or until the precooked crab is heated through, 7 to 10 minutes.

Transfer the crab pieces to a serving platter, surround them with the rosemary sprigs and lemon slices, and serve. Have a discard bowl available for shells, and provide plenty of napkins.

Makes 2 to 4 servings

Cooking with Crab

Buying and Storing Crab

The size restriction on most commercial harvest of Dungeness crab is 6¼ inches from tip to tip on the carapace, which means that the smallest Dungeness that you are likely to see whole at the market will weigh about 1½ pounds. The average size of Dungeness in retail markets is about 2 pounds, and it's not often that you'll see crab much larger than 3 pounds in stores.

When buying a live crab, choose one that is visibly active. Let the professionals drop their arms into those live tanks, but you get to accept or reject their choices. Keep the crab cool in transit (ask for some crushed ice if it's warm out or if you won't be home right

away) and refrigerate it as soon as you get home. Live crab need some air, so open up the packaging a bit and put the crab in a double thickness of plastic bag. I like to clear out a vegetable bin for storing crab, to help contain any leakage from the bags. Live crab will be somewhat dulled by the chill of the refrigerator, so don't expect them to rummage around much in there.

If the recipe you're using calls for crab portions, you might as well save yourself some work and ask the folks at the fish market to clean the crab for you. This is especially true for live crab that you want to roast, stir-fry, or otherwise cook from a raw state. It's a messier and more challenging prospect to clean a live crab than a cooked crab, not for the faint of heart. Most good seafood markets that go to the trouble of supplying crabs from live tanks are willing and able to clean the crab for you.

Live or raw portioned crab should be cooked the same day you purchase it.

For cooked whole crab, look for those without punctures or other breaks in the shell. The crab should feel heavy in your hand, indicating that it is full of moist meat. Check that all ten legs, especially the claws, are intact. Bulk crabmeat should smell sweet and only slightly briny, like the ocean at high tide. Avoid any crabmeat that looks dried out or has a heavy "fishy" aroma. Cooked crab, whether in the shell or not, will keep for a few days if well chilled, but it will be at its best for flavor and moistness if used right away.

Note that the precooked crab sold at stores is fully cooked and ready to eat, or ready to portion and use in a recipe. Try to "cook" this crab only until it is heated through—too much additional cooking and the crab will begin to dry out and lose its flavor.

King crab is almost exclusively sold frozen, aside from a few big-city outlets tapping into the newer trend of selling live kings in tanks. A few stores will cook the crab on-site and sell the legs right away, a treat indeed, though an expensive one. Frozen king leg portions should be individually wrapped and solidly frozen. Carefully check any exposed flesh that's visible: it should not look dry or discolored, which indicates freezer burn or other poor handling. You'll be paying a lot for this crab, so make sure you're getting your money's worth.

Thaw the crab legs in a deep pan (such as an oblong baking dish) in the refrigerator overnight. The crab will give off a lot of water as it thaws, primarily because the legs are generally coated in a thin glaze of ice to protect them, especially from contact with air. I've found a good 20 percent loss from frozen to thawed weight, so if the recipe calls for 1½ pounds thawed king crab, you should purchase about 2 pounds frozen.

Boiling and Steaming Dungeness Crab

You need a big pot to cook whole crab at home, particularly if you're feeding a crowd. When a family crab feed's on the menu, consider using a pot as big as 16 quarts to get through the volume of crabs to keep everyone happy, or have a couple of smaller pots boiling away at the same time. Even for just one crab, at least 8 quarts in volume will be best. Rather than cooking the crab whole, you can instead cook the crab in cleaned halves, which will allow you to fit more crabs into the pot. Cooking crab preportioned and cleaned also leaves the meat more pure-white and slightly milder in flavor, since the yellowish viscera is not in contact with the meat as it is when crab is cooked whole.

To Boil Crab: Fill a large pot with water up to a few inches below the top. Add plenty of salt, about ½ cup per gallon of water. Cover the pot and bring the water to a boil. If boiling a whole live crab, put it in the freezer to chill well and make it docile while the water is heating. (The crab shouldn't actually freeze, so don't leave it in the freezer for more than 15 or 20 minutes.) When the water's at a full rolling boil, carefully but quickly slip the crab into the water headfirst. Cover the pot, return the water to a full boil, then reduce the heat to medium-high so the water's actively gurgling but not boiling over. Cook the crab 18 to 20 minutes for a 2-pound whole crab, about 15 minutes if using cleaned crab portions, counting the time from when the water comes back to a boil. Keep an eye on the pot during cooking; the liquids may bubble up and over the edge, so you might want to set the lid askew to allow some steam to escape.

To Steam Crab: Put 3 to 4 inches of water in a large pot and add a collapsible steamer basket to the bottom of the pot. (If you don't have a steamer basket, you could use a metal colander set in the bottom of the pot, preferably with feet to hold the base above the pot bottom.) Cover the pot and bring the water to a boil over high heat. Sedate the crab in the freezer as noted above. When the water's at a full rolling boil, add the crab to the steamer basket, cover, and steam for about 22 minutes for whole crab, about 18 minutes for crab portions. Keep an eye on the water level during cooking to be certain that the pot doesn't boil dry; if necessary, add a few more cups of very hot (preferably boiling) water.

Drain the cooked crabs in the sink. If serving the crab chilled, run cold water over them or put them in a sink full of ice water to cool quickly, then drain well and refrigerate until ready to serve. Or if serving the crabs hot, give them a quick rinse under cold water and you're ready to go. Either way, before serving whole crabs, follow the cleaning and portioning instructions given below.

Cleaning and Portioning Dungeness Crab

To clean a cooked crab, begin on the underside by lifting up and removing the "apron" or small narrow flap of shell. (This apron, by the way, identifies the crab as a male; on a female crab the apron is quite broad rather than narrow.) Turn the crab over and lift off the carapace (top shell). If you're a fan of crab butter, spoon out the soft, yellowish butter and set it aside in a small dish. Otherwise, discard it with the remaining innards that are tucked in the body cavity. Also lift off the feathery gills that are on either side of the body cavity. Rinse the crab well under cold running water. Use a large heavy knife to cut the body in half where it narrows at the center. If you have a crab, live or precooked, cleaned for you at the market, this is what you'll be taking home.

There are two ways to proceed for portioning, though for a crab feed or other informal meal, you could simply serve the cleaned cooked halves as is. Many cooks pull the legs away from the body, then cut each body half into 2 or 3 pieces. But I prefer a method that leaves some body meat attached to each leg portion. Set the half crab upright on the chopping board with the legs up and the body portion flat on the surface. Using a cleaver or other big sharp, heavy knife (this will not work with a paring knife!), make a swift downward chop between each of the legs, through the soft cartilage of the body. Use whichever method appeals to you.

For precooked crab that is to be used in a recipe, lightly crack the shells of the legs so that flavorings from the other ingredients will more easily penetrate the meat. Use the back of a heavy knife or a wooden mallet and try to avoid crushing the shell into the meat. Ideally, the legs will remain intact.

If you're serving the crab as is, it's ready for the table. Be sure to provide your guests with crab crackers and small seafood forks to make easier work of getting the meat from the shells. When you get to the big luscious claws, the meat will come out easier if you first remove the loose claw joint: just grab that pincer and bend it backwards, pulling it away from the claw. It should come away with a thin membrane that runs down the center of the claw meat. Have a bowl or two on the table for guests to discard shells as they go.

Crab Butter: Crab "butter" is one of those wonderful culinary euphemisms, like sea urchin "roe" (gonads) and sweetbreads (thymus gland . . . but oh so delicious!). This yellow-amber soft material (it's more grayish when raw) is found clinging to the underside of the carapace and in the body cavity of the crab. It is mostly hepatopancreas, an organ that serves a number of purposes for the crab, which includes acting something like our liver. Devotees of crab butter swear by stirring it into sauces to serve with crab or simply eating it as is. But an informal poll of crab lovers found them split on whether they eat crab butter.

Numerous crab festivities are held throughout the Northwest each year. This is just a sampling.

JANUARY

**Mendocino Crab & Wine Days,
Mendocino County, California**

Ten days of events, beginning the last weekend of January through the first weekend of February, do good justice to the crabbing and wine industries in northern California. The festivities are held throughout the county, featuring everything from crab cruises and crabbing demonstrations, cooking demonstrations and winemaker dinners, to "the crabbiest person contest" and other lighter festival fare. For more information, got to www.gomendo.com or call 866-466-3636 (toll-free).

FEBRUARY

**World Championship Crab Races,
Crescent City, California**

This fun community event is held every February, the Sunday before President's Day, an afternoon of wacky crab races with three categories of "jockeys" vying for trophies: children, general public, and groups or organizations. There is also an ongoing crab feed as well as an arts and crafts fair. Crescent City is just south of the Oregon border in the prime crabbing country of Northern California, and this event, which began in 1965, celebrates the region's crab industry. For information, go to www.northerncalifornia.net or call 800-343-8300 (the Crescent City Chamber of Commerce).

**Charleston Merchant's Annual Crab Feed,
Charleston Marina, Oregon**

Generally held on the second Saturday in February, this crab feed has deep community roots, and is sponsored by the merchants association to fund the town's information center. Besides feasting on the season's prime crab, you can join in the merchant's raffle or maybe help judge a children's art show, whatever the planners have up their sleeve for that year. For more information, call the Charleston Marina harbormaster at 541-888-2548 or go to www.portofcoosbay.com.

APRIL

**Westport's Crab Feed & Derby,
Westport, Washington**

The marina in Westport is the place to be on the third weekend of April each year, where fun is had by all in the name of celebrating the region's crab industry. Presented in conjunction with the Washington Dungeness Crab Fisherman's Association, this weekend offers a crab feed and lively crab races on Saturday, with a dance that night sponsored by the WDCFA. Sunday includes other events such as survival suit races for crabbers. Both days, you can join in the crab derby and try for your shot at cash prizes as well as other prizes donated by local businesses. For more information, go to www.westportgrayland-chamber.org or call 800-345-6223.

**The Astoria-Warrenton Crab & Seafood Festival,
Astoria, Oregon**

Held the last full weekend of April each year, this community festival celebrates the region's crabbing traditions with a weekend of continuous entertainment, Oregon wine sampling, and a nonstop crab feed dinner prepared by the Astoria Rotary Club. Crab charters await at the docks to take folks out for a hands-on crabbing experience. For more information, call 503-325-6311 or go to www.oldoregon.com.

MAY

Koniag's Kodiak Crab Festival, Kodiak, Alaska

Late May every year, from the Thursday before Memorial Day through Memorial Day Monday, Kodiak becomes a frenzy of activity during the Kodiak Crab Festival. You'll find a wide variety of events from the blessing of the fleet to a frog-jumping contest, pancake breakfasts to poetry readings. Crab's not as big a focus as you might think, though a couple of vendors serve up fresh crab. There'll be some crabby characters in the grand parade, and you are surrounded by intensive seafood culture. For more information, call 907-486-5557 or go to www.kodiak.org/crabfest.html.

JUNE

Wheeler Crab Fest, Wheeler, Oregon

Held the third weekend of June each year (though best to check in advance because the date varies slightly), this entirely volunteer weekend of festivities features an ongoing crab feed as the main event, with arts and crafts vendors, live music, and other entertainment to make this a full weekend of down-home fun. Just off scenic Highway 101, Wheeler overlooks Nehalem Bay in northwestern Oregon. For more information, go to www.nehalembaychamber.com or call Peg Miller at 503-368-6881.

AUGUST

Crab Bounty Hunt, Winchester Bay, Oregon

For the month of August, crabbing on Winchester Bay might just bring you more than a tasty potful of crabs. At the beginning of the month, 100 legal-size crabs are released into the bay, each with a tag offering instructions on where to register your catch. From those tag numbers, a drawing at the end of the month decides which lucky crabber will go home with the $5,000 pot. For more information, call the Reedsport/Winchester Bay Chamber of Commerce at 800-247-2155.

YEAR-ROUND

The Crab Lab at the Oregon Coast Aquarium, Newport, Oregon

Within the main galleries of this noteworthy aquarium, you can get a close-up look at Dungeness and other crabs, learning about their habitat and life cycle, how they eat, their cousin crabs (such as hermit and rock), and that fascinating process of molting. For more information, call 541-867-3474 or go to www.aquarium.org/crab_lab.htm.

Dungeness Crabbing Adventures at Groveland Cottage B&B, Sequim, Washington

You'll be crabbing on Dungeness Bay itself in the time-honored tradition: wading into the low tide with hip waders, pitchforks for scooping up the crabs, and buckets—all of which the Groveland provides. Winter's best, when low tides at night make easier work of finding the crabs, but excursions can be planned for groups of six or more year-round. For more information, call 800-879-8859 or check out www.sequimvalley.com.

Retail Shops

A few highlights among the top seafood markets in the region are

Longliner Sea Foods Ltd.

Top-quality seafood in the Granville Island
Public Market in Vancouver, B.C.

1689 Johnston Street
Vancouver, B.C. V6H 3R9
604-681-9016

Mutual Fish

Outstanding Seattle seafood retail shop.
2335 Rainier Avenue South
Seattle, Washington 98144
206-322-4368
www.mutualfish.com

Newman's Fish Co.

Select seafood in Portland.

(City Market, Northwest Portland)
735 NW 21st Avenue
Portland, Oregon 97209
503-227-2700

(Eastside)
1403 NE Weidler Avenue
Portland, Oregon 97232
503-284-4537

Pender Seafoods

A bustling Vancouver, B.C., Chinatown market,
especially in the mornings.

284 East Pender, Vancouver
Vancouver, B.C. V6A 1T7
604-687-5946

Uwajimaya

Japanese megagrocer based in Seattle with
excellent seafood and produce departments.

600 Fifth Avenue South
Seattle, Washington 98104
206-624-6248

10500 SW Beaverton-Hillsdale Hwy
Beaverton, Oregon 97005
503-643-4512

15555 NE 24th
Bellevue, Washington 98007
425-747-9012

www.uwajimaya.com

Online Resources

www.alaskaseafood.org

Website for the Alaska Seafood Marketing Institute.

www.ca-seafood.org

The California Seafood Council has unfortunately disbanded, but the website is being maintained for general use and information; includes industry information, seasonality, species profiles, and recipes.

www.dfg.ca.gov

California Department of Fish and Game

www.dfw.state.or.us

Oregon Department of Fish and Wildlife

www.simplyseafood.com

Some of the content from my former days at this magazine (no longer published on paper) is still posted here, including species information, recipes, cooking techniques, etc.; there's also a "seafood superstore" that offers top-quality seafood of all types to consumers around the world, including Alaska king, snow, and Dungeness crab.

www.state.ak.us/adfg/adfghome.htm

Alaska Department of Fish and Game

www.ucinet.com/~dcrab/index.html

Oregon Dungeness Crab Commission's website, including information on the state crabbing industry, nutritional information, recipes, crab biology, and more.

www.wa.gov/wdfw

Washington Department of Fish and Wildlife

INDEX

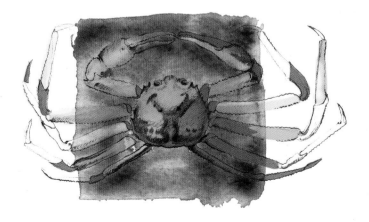